Have you ever asked of these questions?

* How can I make the man I want fall in love with me?

* Why do I always seem to pick the wrong men?

* Why do some Black men seem to totally "lose themselves" to White women?

* What does a Black man really want in bed?

In this second edition of *Get on Top! A Sister's Guide to Life, Love and her Biggest Difficulty...* those questions will be answered and more. *Get on Top!* is a survival manual, a must-have for the conscientious Sister! This book contains tips and techniques for empowerment that have never before been revealed. Turn the pages and discover...

* What the Black man's biggest secret is and how it can affect you. (Page 61)

* How to become a more positive, confident and beautiful Black woman. (Page 133)

* How to quickly spot men that are losers and avoid being set-up by them. (Page 41)

* Ways to make life with your man as exciting as the first time you made love. (Page 111)

And so much more!

This fun, practical and easy-to-follow guide will give you the tools you need to work on every aspect of your personal life. Most importantly, you will gain control over the most difficult thing you will ever have to deal with...

A Sister's Guide to Life, Love and her Biggest Difficulty...

Get on Top!
(and Stay There!)
A Sister's Guide to Life, Love and her Biggest Difficulty...

The Righteous Mother

© 1997, 1999 by The Righteous Mother
First Printing 1997
Second Printing 1999, revised
Excerpts and Introduction © 1997, 1999 by Sister Shakeefa
Book design and illustrations by Cleopatra
Cover illustration by Craig Rippon

Published by:

 Swing Street
Box #846, Cathedral Station
New York, NY 10025-0846 USA

Library of Congress Catalog Card Number: 98-60121

ISBN: 0-9652540-2-X 9.95

Prepared with the support and assistance of
New Youth in Movement
and Groovy Move, Inc.

Printed in The United States of America

This book is dedicated to the one million Black men who made history on October 16, 1995 when they assembled peacefully and marched on our nation's capital under the supervision of Minister Louis Farrakhan. Without men like these, there would be no hope for the future.

Acknowledgments

The Righteous Mother would like to thank the following:
Sister Shakeefa, for having a vision, sharing it with me and making a lifelong dream a reality, Cleopatra, for her wonderful artwork, my family, especially my children for understanding and supporting what I have set out to accomplish, my grandchildren, for making me laugh when I truly needed it, Swing Street Publishing, for believing in me and giving me the opportunity to share my knowledge and you, the reader for taking the time to see what I have to offer.

Sister Shakeefa thanks:
Renee, Marce, D-Strong, Butch, Thit and Tottie, nothin' but love for ya! "Kit", my favorite aunt, "Lo-Jo" and "Dugga", just for being themselves, D.J., "The Gott-Man and Willster", for keeping me company on so many nights in front of the computer, Charles, a.k.a. "The Beast", G.E., for listening to me when I needed an ear, advising me and being a friend and Swing Street Publishing, for taking a chance and investing in what I know will be a successful project.

Cleopatra thanks:
God, for loving, guiding and protecting me every step of the way. My mother, without whom, my life would not have been possible. You are my best friend and I love you. Thanks, mom.

The publisher would like to thank the following:
New Youth in Movement, Craig Rippon, Chuck Williams, Aldo Sampiero, "Teach", Dorcas Meyers and all of our friends, and supporters. Last but not least, we wish to thank you, the most important person of all... our reader.

Our apologies to anyone we may have missed. Although you were not mentioned, you still have our sincere gratitude.

CONTENTS

INTRODUCTION

by Sister Shakeefa

Dear Black Sister:

Welcome! Welcome to a whole new realm of knowledge, insight and understanding! Now that you've taken the first step by buying this book, get ready for some terrific changes in your life! *Get on Top! (and Stay There!) A sister's guide to Life, Love and her Biggest Difficulty...* is the only book of its kind. It was written by Black women, for Black women, about the issues Black women face. This book is not for the squeamish! It is raw and it is truthful. It is a work that is considered by many to be long overdue. Others fear its powerful message, yet find themselves drawn to it just the same. It is here for your own personal benefit and interpretation. Derive from it what you will. And may the power of positive thinking be with you.

Some time ago, a book was written for Black men that unjustly held Black women responsible for all of Black men's problems. The book, written by a Black Muslim woman, has gone on to create further difficulties for Sisters already in hardship. The "Guide" for Black men says we (Black women) are to blame for everything, including a Black man's own deficiencies and it encourages Brothers to treat us in ways that are beneath us. Our men have even been advised to hit us! As I'm sure you'll agree, we Sisters have a different story to tell. Black women are not mindless animals in need of dominance, humiliation and cruelty in order to function properly, we are women in need of love, honor and respect. We are women who love our men and are desperately trying to save our families. We are women who have been stifled throughout history in every way, subjected to constant struggle and abuse. We have been forced to hold our tongues, even when we've known the true answer. Not anymore. Now, we have a voice. Through our book, **Get on Top!** every Black Woman with courage can finally speak. And it's about time the truth be spoken. And heard. What will it take for our Brothers to listen?

Just about everything you'll ever need to deal with your life and interpersonal relationships is contained in this one volume. And everything you need to know about the Black man will be told to you. As you read on, you'll understand why this is the book some Black men do not want you to ever read.

As you progress to each new chapter, apply what you are learning and you will see immediate improvement in your everyday situations. The Black man will no longer be your biggest difficulty. When you have finished reading this book, recommend it to a friend or pass it on so that another Sister can benefit from the infinite wisdom contained here. The Righteous Mother has blessed us with enlightenment!

In the meantime, Peace, Health and best of Luck in your relationships! It's time we start givin' 'em Hell! Stay strong!

 Love, Sister Shakeefa
❋

Why We Need This Book!
By Sister Shakeefa

What you are about to read will explain why we need this book. We begin by treating you to...

A FEW WORDS FROM SOME OF OUR BLACK MEN

The following are excerpts of actual live interviews. Uncut and uncensored. Proceed at your own discretion.

BROTHER #1

Name: Crowbar

A.K.A: Toudlum Johnson

Occupation: Mental Health Administrator and Independent Entrepreneur. Also an aspiring "Pharmacist."

In other words: Crack Dealer

Place of employment: Any available street corner.

Job Duties: The development and manufacture of Crack Cocaine, sales and marketing, collection procedures for delinquent accounts, local terrorism.

Age: Unknown.

Special interests: Looking important and getting pussy.

Here's what Crowbar had to say...

"Why do I sell Crack? Because my mama ain't give me a goddamn thing. I gotta go out there and take what I want. Our Black leaders ain't shit trying to lead you to McDonald's and minimum wage. I ain't tryin' to work for no minimum wage, not when I can get mine straight up in the streets. I'm tryin' to make loot. ...I roll with some crazy notorious mothafuckas. Niggas that ain't got no feelings. Niggas that be killin' Nigga's fathers and got bodies up under their belt. You know what I'm sayin'? You ain't a real man until you got a body up under your belt."

We asked Crowbar what his views were about women. Check out his response.

"If I put a bitch down, I don't take her out and I don't give her no money. Once you start givin' a bitch money, they try and do what the fuck they wanna do. I tell her straight up; "Look Baby, I'm riskin' my life and my freedom to get this loot. I ain't tryin' to trick it on no bitch. You want us to go out, that shit got to be on you." Fuck taking bitches out to dinner. I be crackin' for that ass while their stomachs growlin'."

BROTHER #2

Name : Ant

A.K.A : Anthony Smith

Occupation : Diversified Public facilitator

In other words: Bum

Place of employment : Anywhere there's an opportunity to make quick money.

Job duties: Washing cars, acting as gopher and pitcher for drug dealers, loading crates, shoveling snow and anything else for five dollars.

Special interests: Hanging out, getting high and getting pussy. He has a pigeon coop on the roof of an abandoned building. Sometimes he sells the pigeons to neighborhood bodegas. He is also a proud, self-proclaimed Ebonics expert.

Age : 36

Listen to what Ant had to say...

"You gotta snatch females up when they're real young. You know, fifteen or sixteen. I don't want no bitch that's been through the mill. Once you put those young shorties down, they be doin' what you say. You train 'em. Once they be following everything you tell 'em, you put a baby up in 'em, 'cause you know once they drop that baby, they ain't like no old bitch that's gonna be fucked up. Their bodies bounce back real quick and they still be lookin' butter."

We asked about the girl he has living in his mother's house. The girl just turned eighteen and already has a child from him.

"I snatched Charla up when she was crazy young, sixteen years old, in high school, but she was the bomb. I could see she was a up and comin' shortie. When we was first seeing her comin' up the block, she'd be walkin' with her bookbag, a good little schoolgirl and we're chillin' out, bumpin' Cracks, making our packages and all that and I'm like, Yo, man. Fuck that. I should snatch that young girl up and put her down with me. And that's what I did."

"But that young girl is somebody's daughter!" Our interviewer, a woman, exclaimed.

"You're mistaking me for somebody that gives a shit." He calmly replied. He later tried to rap to the interviewer. Ugh!

BROTHER #3

Name: Jesse Mack

Alias: None

Occupation: Transit worker

Job Duties: Selling subway tokens

Special interests: Rap music, going to the gym and getting pussy. Occasionally, he likes to see a live basketball game.

Age: 28

"Black women are fucked up. That's why I prefer to fuck with Spanish women. At least they listen to what you tell them. They don't be with that dumb shit. A lot of Black women are all about money. I ain't working my ass off to give no bitch no money. Niggers that give women money are suckers. A Black woman'll try and pimp a nigger."

We asked him what he thought about marriage. He laughed.

"Nigger got to be crazy! Not with all this pussy floatin' around. Let those other stupid niggers marry the hoes. I'm the fuckin' milk man. I'll come by and hit 'em with dick when they ain't gettin' it, when their niggers get tired of that pussy, 'cause every nigger gonna get tired of that pussy sooner or later. I be tearin' their asses up and sending them home to their husbands and boyfriends. Freaks love this big, Black nigger."

Ironically, Jesse is an only son. He has several sisters, all of which are married with children. Jesse has no children of his own. He was born in the South and raised in New York. His parents are divorced.

BROTHER #4

Name: Darryl Carter

Occupation: Account executive

Age: 34

Special interests: Marathon running, watching videos, cooking gourmet dinners and getting pussy from White girls.

Get ready for Darryl's view:

"I like all types of women, but I prefer to date White women. I don't see any reason why I should have to date Black women just because I'm Black. All of the Black women I've dated were screwed up in one way or another. I'm not here to be a sociologist or a substitute for someone's daddy. I need a real woman. And until I find a Black woman that can fit into that category, I'm going to continue dating White girls."

THE MAN WE CALL "BROTHER #5"

Name: "Lorenzo"

Occupation: Former professional athlete, currently investing in Mutual Funds.

Age: 48

Special Interests: Restoring antiques, earning dividends, looking and feeling important and of course, getting pussy.

"I'm so sick of hearing these women complain about how men are dogs, etc. We couldn't be dogs if there weren't women out there encouraging us. Most of the women I meet are interested in what they can get out of me because of my fame and the money I have. That's why I dog them. When I meet a woman, I don't waste my time trying to get to know her. I just want the pussy and that's it. Get in and get out. I don't have the time or the energy to get involved. Besides that, there are just too many women out there. Why bother?"

Note: Whenever Lorenzo meets a new woman, he gives her an autographed photo of himself from the cover of an obscure 1970 sports magazine. Talk about living in the past! He's based in Chicago, hangs out in L.A. and constantly tries to rub elbows with celebrities. He harps over the perks he feels he deserved, but never received as an athlete and brags to anyone who will listen. He is sure everyone recognizes him and thinks he needs a body guard. However, his career as a celebrity is limited to meager appearances dressed as a potato chip bag at supermarket openings and commentating at charity ball games with no media coverage. He still wears those bell-bottomed, polyester trousers that hook at the waistline. He also does "The Funky Chicken" at parties with a proud smile on his face.

Do you now see why we need this book?

It's difficult to believe there are actually Black men who think and act like those mentioned. But, the fact is, a number of Black men do. And we're sure that as a Black woman, you've had to deal with them at one time or another. But, before you write all of the Brothers off, remember the million African-American men that marched on Washington with Minister Farrakhan. Despite the ones who are a waste of time, a number of Black men are keeping it real. By the time you finish reading this book, you'll know how to go about finding them.

So, read on...

* For some insightful information on the types of Black men featured in this chapter, turn to page 71 and the chapter entitled; *The Sucker Syndrome*.

The Black Male Machine:

How does he operate?

He's stubborn, egotistical and hard to understand. On the flip side, he's exciting, strong and comforting to be near. How can a Black man be so irresistible one minute and then disgust you the next? The answer lies in his programming.

Real man or Robot?

Is your man a real man, or is he a "robot"? Take this simple true or false test and find out.

	TRUE	FALSE
1. Your man has bad habits he just can't seem to break.	____	____
2. Even if your man knows he's wrong, he just can't admit it.	____	____
3. Your man has a tendency to want sex at around the same time of day or during the same days of the week.	____	____
4. Your man has trouble opening up to new ideas.	____	____
5. Your man has to do everything *his* way.	____	____

Real man or Robot?   TRUE   FALSE

6. When you try to give your
   man advice, he gets upset.   _____   _____

7. Your man seems like he can't
   help but stare at a woman
   with a big ass.   _____   _____

8. When you catch your man
   staring at another woman's
   ass, he swears he wasn't
   and really seems to mean it.   _____   _____

9. Your man thinks he's the best
   lover in the world.   _____   _____

10. Your man always shows off
    in front of his friends and
    acts macho in the presence
    of other women.   _____   _____

Now, tally up your answers.

If you answered "True" to seven (7) or more statements, your man is a robot. He will act as programmed and find it difficult to bypass his fixed circuitry. Many Black men are like this, but don't despair. There are ways to deal with them.

LEARNING TO DEAL WITH THE ROBOT

Why are some Black men like robots?

There are several reasons why a Black man may be like a robot. First of all, it's easier to be a robot. Robots are not required to *think*. Aside from having Robotics as part of his basic personality, a man can become programmed for cyborg behavior in many different ways.

Maybe it's due to his family upbringing. It could be that he's not *intelligent* enough to break away from the programming. He could be that way as a result of his experiences. It may even be hereditary: based on genetics! One thing is certain: the more ignorant a Black man is, the more robotic he tends to be. When a man is a robot, he'll always respond to the same things in the same way at the same time. He processes data like a machine. His behavior will be methodical and predictable. He honestly can't help it.

Have you ever wondered how most men can sit in front of the television on a Sunday afternoon and watch one sports game after the other, all day long? If there are five basketball games on that day, they could watch every one and never leave the couch except to get a beer or go to the bathroom. That's because in sports, everything follows a format, plan or structure. Robots love structure.

Have you ever noticed how a man can eat the same foods all the time as long as they taste okay? This type of man has no imagination and doesn't want one. He's a robot. If you are with a man like this, you probably find yourself being the one to suggest eating out. And when you do go out, it has to be to a restaurant he already knows. And he'll order the same thing!

He buys the same kinds of clothes, cuts his hair in the same style at the same barber shop and wears the same cologne. All of his underwear are identical. Try and explain something to him and watch how baffled he gets. Listen to him talk. Always the same shit.

Day in and day out, he lectures you, even when he doesn't know what he's talking about! What about fixing things? He can fix anything (or, so he thinks)! You couldn't possibly tell him how to do it. After all, you're just a woman. And the man really knows what's best. *He's the one with the penis!*

The penis: what a powerful, yet marvelous tool! His penis is the master and he is the slave. It commands and he obeys. Anytime his dick gets hard, he reacts. He can't help himself. He's good in bed, can be fantastic even, but he always does it the same way in the same positions. He's got his own special flavor and doesn't want to change the taste. He's on a routine.

He may be a perfectly synchronized machine, but he's still a robot. And he can get on your nerves.

So what's a woman to do?

The good thing about a robot is it can be reprogrammed. This is assuming he doesn't have some defect. A robot with a defect is virtually impossible to change. Men also have varying degrees of "The Robot Factor." If your robot is a normal robot, there may be hope. The key to improving a robot is not to let the robot know of your intentions. Robots are very sensitive. For more information on reprogramming your robot, read on. You have chosen the right book to aid you in your quest! With a bit of common sense, luck and enlightenment, you can achieve your goal. There *is* a way to turn your robot into a real man! Fortunately, whatever assistance you may need will be available in the chapters to come. Good luck!

ONLY JOKING

Question: Why should there be female astronauts?

Answer: When the crew gets lost in space, at least the woman will ask for directions.

Who are you Making Love To?

Write "Yes" or "No" next to each question in every answer group.

Is, or Does your Man...

Group A

- Into Physical fitness?
- Mr. Fix it?
- Eat healthy foods?
- Bald headed?
- Aged 25-40?
- Drive a jeep?
- Play a sport?
- Wear a baseball cap?
- Drink Heineken beer?

Group B

- Like to sing
- Wear a tie in his leisure time?
- Go to church/pray on a regular basis?
- An intellectual?
- Have an analytical mind?
- Live in the suburbs?
- Wear a goatee?
- Eat chitterlings?
- Drive a Japanese car?

Group C

- Wear neon colors?
- Have an exotic pet?
- Drive recklessly?
- In, or was in the military?
- Awkward?

- Wear a funky/punk haircut?
- Listen to Rock music or Opera?
- Wear stripes, plaids or patterns on a regular basis?
- Sleep with his eyes open?

Group D

• Have poor personal hygiene?

• Tend to be cheap?

• Tattoo his body?

• Pierce his body?

• Wear black often?

• A heavy drug user?

• Have a criminal record?

• Like to gamble?

• Have gold teeth?

Group E

• A couch potato?

• Hate to exercise?

• Eat a lot of junk food?

• Overweight or in poor physical shape?

• Live in a hi-rise apartment?

• Drink two six-packs?

• Have a really full beard?

• Work for the government?

• Keep a remote in his hand?

Group F

• Drive a sports car?

• Like to give lectures?

• Spend a lot of time on the telephone or cellular?

• Drive a late-model car?

• Love to travel?

• Wear a Wet Curl?

• Eat a lot of candy?

• Sniff or smoke cocaine?

• Work in real estate?

Group G

• Ride a motorcycle or bike?

• A video arcade addict?

• Aged 17-24?

• Live with relatives/friends?

• Refuse to get a job?

• In debt or have bad credit?

• Eat a lot of snack food?

• Change philosophies often?

• Always have his male friends hanging around?

Group H

- Get regular manicures?

- Relax his hair?

- Have photos of himself all around his apartment?

- Constantly in the mirror?

- Wear earrings in both ears?

- Wear a lot of gold jewelry?

- Wear bikini briefs?

- Think or know he has a big beautiful penis?

- Want to be a star?

Group I

- A good dancer?

- Drive a luxury car?

- Have his finances in order?

- Play a musical instrument?

- Sleep on his back?

- Like to spend money?

- Lotion his skin?

- Have a playful, sarcastic way about him?

- Have a deep voice?

Now, let's find out what all of this means...

Begin with the questions in Group A. Count all of your "Yes" answers. If you answered "Yes" to more than six questions, it's time to find out: Is your man a Slam Master? See page 14.

Now, move to the questions in Group B. How many "Yes" answers? If there are more than six, your man could be a Smooth Operator. Page 15.

What about Group C? More than six "Yes" answers could mean he's a truly original lover. Find out how original. Pages 16-19. See: Side-Winder, Humpty Dumpty and Contortionist.

In this world, there are Backstabbers, Freaks and Beasts. More than six "Yes" answers in Group D? Turn to pages 16, 20, 21.

In Group E, six out of nine "Yes" answers show if your man is a Flatliner or a Noodle. If he is, he's on pages 18 and 22.

Six out of nine "Yes" answers in group F could be significant. Your man might have a nice piece of wood, but only because he's a Woodpecker. Read all about him on page 20.

How sexually articulate is your man? Six "Yes" responses in Group G might tell you. Turn to "The Apprentice" on page 22.

They say "The King" is not dead! Perhaps that's why there are so many Elvis Impersonators. Are you involved with one? More than six "Yes" answers in Group H? Look at page 23.

There's a man who's the cream of the crop and his name is Mr. Magic. In order for your man to earn this prestigious title, you must have at least five "Yes" answers in Group I as well as in Groups A and B. Turn to page 24, lick your lips and keep your fingers crossed!

Different Strokes

Many experts believe a man's lovemaking style can be a true indicator of his personality. A Black man may change his sexual approach according to his mood, but most Brothers have a standard method of making love that works for them.

THE SLAM MASTER

A hard-core, satisfying lover, the Slam Master loves to slam no matter what time of day or night. He will slam you without end, sometimes until you have a stomach ache. He can fuck non-stop for hours. Although he makes grunting noises, often like an animal and ending up sweaty, he can still be tremendously sexy. He will leave you feeling really sore around the edges. The Slam Master often has fantastic arm muscles. They're what enable him to do those push ups in the missionary position. He's often powerful enough to pick you up and do it to you against a wall. He'll make you feel very feminine and helpless.

He may also like to display his strength in other situations, removing beer bottle caps with his teeth and breaking wood with his hands. He's a brute of a man and loves when you show appreciation for his machismo. When making love, the Slam Master stares into space. That's because he's concentrating. Let him concentrate. He's usually not a man of many words. The taller he is, the more slamming power he should have. Don't get us wrong. A shorter man can slam, too. But, if you make love to a Brother over six feet tall who is lacking slamming power, there may be something seriously wrong. Suggestions: Write him letters telling him how proud you are of his slamming ability. Never complain when he wants to go to the gym. A Slam Master has to work out and pump weights regularly. Encourage him. You want him to slam you on the regular for as long as you're together.

THE SMOOTH OPERATOR

Like that song, there's no need to ask. The Smooth Operator reaches and maintains an even, slow rhythm. What more can a woman in love or in lust want? The Smooth Operator lives to savor the pussy. He moans, groans and sighs a lot. He loves to caress and kiss. He may get there slowly, but when he does, he really makes an arrival. The Smooth Operator always wants to make love after he finishes a good meal. Food is an aphrodisiac for him, as long as he doesn't overeat. He's a simple, down-home, old-fashioned kind of guy.

He may have a slight Southern accent, or have family from the South, be of stout build and have very full lips. He's often sensuous looking with beguiling, brown eyes. He may also have a fat or round stomach, but don't let that bother you. It's part of his overall appeal. He usually eats slow, talks slow and works slow, but he gets the job done. He loves to listen to the smooth R&B crooners, sometimes those male groups from the sixties. He may have facial hair or hair on his chest, love fried chicken and adore Teddy Pendergrass' old songs and singers like Aaron Hall and R. Kelly.

Suggestions: Cook him delicious meals whenever he comes home. Buy him a CD of his favorite hits and play it while making love. That should get him rolling.

Extra note: Studies have shown that some men get horny smelling cinnamon rolls. No kidding! The smell of cinnamon seems to turn them on. Imagine what fresh-baked cinnamon rolls from your oven will do for a Smooth Operator! Hint hint!

THE SIDE-WINDER

Now, this guy is original. He loves to hit it at an angle. For some reason, it just feels better to him that way. It might feel good to you, too. From the side, on a diagonal, flip it over and around from the left... can that man make things bounce! One thing: check to see if his penis is curved. Why? That may explain why he's a Side-Winder. He may dress funny, wearing odd colors and clothes that are a touch too large or too small. He may like to roller skate. If he's of higher intelligence, he will be inclined to go into law or medicine.

In bed, he can last a good while, but his sexual technique may cause pain on occasion. He often gets off by pinching nipples and biting. You may also catch him sleeping with his eyelids parted. When a Side-Winder kisses, his tongue can move really fast. He might like to lick your teeth and put his tongue in your ear. He may also use Zen Focus on you to stare you down. If you make love to a Side-Winder, notice what side he tends to lean to. As a child, he may have been hit upside the head too many times, probably on the same side of his head.

Suggestions: Alternate sides during sex. You don't want to end up with a tilted uterus.

THE BACK STABBER

As the name implies, this man loves to do it from the back.

For the life of him, he loves to look at ass. Be wary. He may sometimes want to disassociate himself from you. That could be why he always wants to do it without ever seeing your face or kissing you. All men love to do it doggie-style, but damn, there is a limit. The Back stabber may have trouble expressing himself and have dog mentality. He could also be fantasizing about your anus. Watch out! He may try to stick it in there on the sneak tip.

Back Stabbers eat a lot of spicy foreign food and shellfish. They also love to drink milkshakes. Many successful actors are Back Stabbers. It could be that many of them have engaged in homosexual activities in order to get roles. If the man you're dealing with is a Back Stabber, he may be untrustworthy. Like that old popular song about backstabbers, he'll "smile in your face", etc. Or, he'll never be able to stare you in the eyes. A normal man will want to experience sex with you in different ways and in different positions. If this guy only gets turned on by doggie style, he's not the one to turn your back on when you're out of bed.

Suggestions: Keep your feelings in serious check. He has the capacity to hurt you. When making love, tell him you can't climax that way. Or, tell him you like to watch him while he's doing it. Gas his head by saying he looks so good when he's pumping and you've just got to see his face. If that doesn't work, yawn when he stays behind you too long. When it's over and he asks you how it was, tell him it could've been better and tell him why. Also, guard your anus with your life!

THE HUMPTY DUMPTY

Has no real rhythm or technique, but loves to bounce. You could be dry and disinterested, but he'll still keep on humping. He's like a "Rock 'em, Sock 'em Robot", or a squeaky toy with springs. He can't dance, or keep a rhythm. He has a lopsided sense of humor, crooked teeth and hangs out on the far side. He may be fun at first, but he can end up being boring. The Humpty Dumpty sometimes lives in a fantasy world. He'll wear punk rock glasses and try to be original, but come off as being weird. He's easily brainwashed and may therefore be a former Marine. He has heavy military mentality.

Humpties usually don't like to eat coochie either. They might do it because they know they'd better, but they'll look like they're being tortured. The Humpty lacks coordination and is not really in tune with his own body. He may wear those canvas, high-top sneakers that come in black, white and orange. He may have several brothers and look nothing like them: the odd man out. The best way to spot a Humpty is by examining his walk. Just like that little egg man who fell off the wall, Mr. Dumpty can't keep his balance. He's frequently tripping over his own two feet.

Suggestions: Calm him down by giving him a few beers before sex. If you're doing the missionary, lock your legs around his back, grind your heels into his butt and force him to keep a logical beat. Keep plenty of AstroLube or comparable lubricant handy for those dry moments. See if you can coax him into giving you some decent oral sex by putting honey, whipped cream or another tasty treat on your vagina.

THE FLATLINER

In medical terms, a "flat liner" is someone who has been classified as medically dead. No heartbeat. No brain waves. Nada. In sexual terms, there's not much difference. Like the cadaver on a slab in the morgue, a man who is a "flatliner" lays there, with you on top and does essentially nothing. He's basically dead. No work for him today, he just wants to relax and enjoy it. He needs to be embalmed. A flatliner doesn't believe in doing what a man should do in bed (ie: push up on his arms and slam) and he doesn't see anything wrong with it. He figures if he has a sizable organ, he can just get hard and let you do the rest. Boy, is he disillusioned. Black men who are flatliners tend to approach life with the same cavalier attitude: not much concern for appearances. Brothers who work in jobs where they sit all day (Middle-aged bus drivers, desk security guards, etc.) are occasional flatliners.

Suggestions: Slap his thighs and tell him he'd better move that ass. Put him on a diet. Encourage him to do push-ups. Buy him some Irish Moss or some Yohimbine.

THE CONTORTIONIST

If you ever meet a man who turns out to be a sexual contortionist, get ready for a totally unique experience. This man will amaze you. He may not blow your socks off, but he will inspire awe. He's a sexual acrobat. When making love, this man puts his body into positions that are way beyond your imagination. Don't ask us how he does it. He's flexible, strong and long lasting. His love muscle is exceptionally hard. You'll definitely like that part. He usually has a fat tongue and/or a long tongue. He'll perform oral sex, but it may not be his specialty. Banging you out is his main priority. He may have studied martial arts. He'll make funny noises while he's doing it and won't stay in one position too long. You may end up having to train him because as soon as you get your swerve on in one position, he'll be pestering you to shift into another. He'll be a lot of fun if you can keep up with him. Young police officers and men with funny shaped heads can often be Contortionists. Men who are into Shiatsu massage and aroma-therapy are somtimes wannabees, meaning, they try to do that contortionist thing to impress you, but they can't sustain it.

Suggestions: If you have an authentic contortionist on your hands, start doing calisthenics on a regular basis. You need to

be in serious shape to deal with this guy. Yoga, anyone?
Extra note: A Cortortionist is even more fun on a waterbed.

THE WOODPECKER

Like that little bird named Woody, this man does not shut up.
In bed, he'll make more noise than you do and get off on it:
moaning and groaning in your ear, whispering, screaming,
asking you to scream, asking you what's his name, calling
your name, calling his mother's name, mumbling things you
don't understand, telling you what to say, this man could
ultimately get on your nerves. The irony is, the sex is often
good, so you keep doing it with him and find yourself just
blocking him out. Does he think all that noise really turns you
on? The woodpecker will make so much of a commotion,
after a while you'll wish you could be screwing *yourself* to see
what the big deal is. Don't let him annoy you. His quirk is
only that he likes to hear himself. It sets him off: like a double
psychological twist in his head. He's in his own special world.
   Suggestions: Blast music while making love to him. Give
him a piece of bubble gum just before sex. It's hard to chew,
breathe and talk at the same time. If that doesn't work, put one
of your nipples in his mouth.

THE FREAK

He's sleazy. "Scuzzy." Unprincipled. But, he looks good.
The Freak may have a shady undertone in his personality that
does or doesn't excite you. He lacks sexual etiquette and may
ask you to do things you find distasteful. He sometimes has
excessively oily skin and may look a little "sweet", if you get
the drift. He may be an erotic dancer in his spare time, a singer
or an actor. There's a definite possibility he's bisexual.
   Despite that, he can get lost in pussy for hours. His cock is

like a hot spear... stabbing you and stabbing you. That part can actually be all right. He'll eat any and every woman's coochie. We're not sure if that's particularly desirable. One man we interviewed who is a self-declared freak said he once ate a woman out for so long, he fell asleep in her crotch. When he and the woman woke up, his crusty face was buried in her pubic hair! If you end up in bed with The Freak, you'll be able to tell right away by the foul language he uses. He's a vulgar man and proud of it. Kissing him may feel nasty. He also has a real fascination with ass. (By the way, we mean *Ass*. For real. Ass, like, in some serious anal activities.)

Suggestions: Keep reliable condoms handy at all times. And use a spermicide, too. You need that added assurance. In fact, use two condoms if you can! Also, you might not want to tell The Freak your real name, or have him visit you at home. He's better suited for short-stay motels. Note: The Freak really gets around and has a tendency to brag about all the pussy he gets.

Warning: He doesn't hesitate to drop names.

THE BEAST

For some reason, maybe even unknown to him, this man likes to make sex painful. For you, that is. He's not a full-fledged sadist, it's not like he sets out to have you in pain all night. He actually thinks you enjoy it that way. And some women do. He'll ram his thick fingers into you while you're still dry and suck your private parts with so much force, they'll feel like they're about to burst. He'll lock onto you like a pit bull.

He can be a real physical specimen; huge muscles, fine face, the whole nine yards, or he can be your average, run of the mill guy. Some men that are "Beasts" like to watch violent films. One "Beast" we know watched the film "Faces of Death" eleven times. Beasts are intense, brooding characters. For some reason, many of them fantasize about Asian women.

It's difficult to advise you on this one. If The Beast really

hurts you, sit down and discuss it with him. Try not to do this on a full moon. If you have no choice other than to do it on a night when the moon is full, load your gun with silver bullets first. Keep it cocked and hidden. Slowly and gently tell The Beast women are sensitive beings and he can't manhandle your clitoris. Watch his face very closely. If he starts to sprout fangs and turn on you, aim for the head and shoot!
P.S. Even garlic and crosses don't work on this guy!

THE NOODLE

If you've ever come in contact with The Noodle, you know what real disappointment is. The guy is totally limp. Granted, his penis can get firm, but it's never bone-hard and it won't stay up for very long. When it comes to making things move, this man has no real strength in his thrust. Is it because of his brain, or his body? We're still trying to figure this one out.

One thing we've noticed about The Noodle is, he usually has a weak handshake. He has a soft voice and a gentle manner. He's also very passive. He says "yes" to everything. If you end up in bed with him, you will often find yourself straining to feel his penis deeper inside you. It can become truly aggravating. The most amazing part is, The Noodle can have a sizable piece of meat. Why then, can't you really feel it?

Suggestions: You get on top. Put a pillow under his butt and instruct him to move his hips. This way, you can get up there and try to wax it. Some Irish Moss or Yohimbine may also do him good. Cayenne Pepper in food has been known to get a man's libido going. Got any Ginseng? Also try giving him a high potency multi-vitamin or a super protein power drink.

THE APPRENTICE...

Most often a young man with little experience or limited insight, The Apprentice has a clumsy but charming way of making love. He'll tend to stumble on things you like by experimenting and will be very open to suggestions you make (unless he's an older man with some ego problems). He hasn't had a large number of quality experiences. When it comes to oral sex, he may fall short. Be patient. This might sound funny, but The Apprentice could be genuinely scared of eating the coochie. As soon as he sees it, his heart palpitates, sweat forms on his brow and he feels like he's about to be swallowed alive. You'll know he's afraid by the way he stares at it whenever he gets close. He thinks it's a ravenous, deadly abyss. Have pity on him. Or, get him drunk. It may make him more receptive.

On the other hand, he may really like the taste. In this case, you're extremely lucky. The Apprentice can be a great lover if he's smart enough to pay attention to what's going on. He'll call you at all hours of the night and ring your bell unexpectedly. If you have a steady man, he could cause problems.

If he's a baby tenderoni, his head can be out in space. He'll probably live with his mother and/or have no real money. He will get very hard, do it several times and always be ready for some fun. Sounds like a go-ahead, right? Don't run out and find him just yet. The Apprentice can be unpredictable and disappear from your life without warning. Just when you need him most, he'll vanish without a trace, leaving you totally confused. And horny. He's best only for an occasional fix.

Suggestions: If you've got a good "Apprentice" and want to keep sleeping with him, find out where he lives so you can track him down whenever you want him. Keep loose change handy in case he needs money to take the bus home. Don't expect much from the relationship and try not to get too attached to the sex. Also avoid his mother. She won't like you.

THE ELVIS IMPERSONATOR

(The King): The King needs to take off his crown and get real! If you want a man you can worship in bed, he's the one.

He will be selfish, uncompromising and for most women, a genuine disappointment. But, he'll be one of the best looking guys you've ever slept with. The King may have everything it takes to satisfy you, including a hefty penis, but the pleasure will fall short because of his ego. He thinks he's the greatest, so why should he listen to what you say? His kiss is cool and impersonal. His hands will grope you with a certain degree of knowledge, after all, he's slept with a lot of women, but you won't find any real feeling there. He's used to having females at his command. He believes you are there to serve him. He will pump adequately, but will not take the time to explore other important areas. He will not perform oral sex on you, but will expect you to do it to him. You will do everything his way, enjoy what he does and never ask questions. He'll want to do it in front of a mirror so he can see himself! This kind of guy will never improve in bed because he's too hung up on his looks and has a steady flow of women to reinforce his already inflated ego. He's usually only good for a one shot deal. Athletic jocks and bodybuilders are often Elvis Impersonators between the sheets.

Suggestions: Hit it, quit it, forget it. If he's a professional athlete or a celebrity, place him as a notch on your belt and move on with pride. The sex will never get any better. Not only that, he'll most likely be unfaithful. He doesn't respect women. So, try not to ever fall in love with him.

MR. MAGIC

Finally, the one we've all been waiting for! This man has it all: stamina, strength, sensitivity, sensuality and most of all, a wonderfully-sized penis. He looks good to you and knows how to push those buttons. There's not much else to say. Mr. Magic will drive you out of your mind with his knowing hands, probing lips and devilish tongue. Sex with him is like a dream come true. He'll masturbate you mentally. You will adore him. No diggity. He's a modest man, he doesn't brag about his sexual prowess because he doesn't have to. Mr. Magic never makes promises he can't keep. His body is pumping and his slammability factor is a 10+. Lips like butter and hands like fire, he's good in any position, at any time of day and is ready whenever you are. Each lovemaking session is a new and wonderful experience. This is one man who's never boring and he always makes you feel like a woman. There's only one problem with Mr. Magic and it's a major one: He's so good in bed, he has the potential to turn you into a deeply disturbed and perpetually horny female. You may become preoccupied with him because you'll be so afraid of losing him. If you get the impression he may be leaving you, you'll want to shoot him.

Suggestions: Attach a ball and chain to his leg and hire a private detective to watch him night and day. Keep close tabs on his penis and make sure it's always worked to the bone.

Mr. Magic should be so sexed out in your care, he'll be too tired to give it to anybody else. Beware: If another woman ever gets a hold of him, you can be sure she'll never go away and she'll make your life miserable.

THE COMBO

Your man is classified as "The Combo" if you answered more than four questions with "Yes" in several groups. The Combo is an interesting man because he can either be pleasing to all women, or pleasing to none. He is most likely capricious, flighty and unpredictable. At the same time, his openness and flexibility can be a plus. If you like adventure, he is probably the man for you. The Combo tends to metamorphose with each new woman. He is usually willing to try new things and will rarely turn his nose up at any suggestion you make. He doesn't fall into any one category and prides himself on being unique. In order to figure out this man, you will need to study your answers carefully. Correlate your findings with the numerous descriptions in this chapter. Within no time at all, you'll know exactly where your lover man is "coming" from. Make him come to you! And have fun!

Whatever kind of man you have, it is your responsibility to get what you need from your sexual relationship. Most men do want to please, as long as they feel their efforts are appreciated. Don't be afraid to ask for what you want. But, remember to ask. Don't demand. And ask him what you can do to make it better for him. Communication improves everything and a man who cares will try his best to thrill you.

Why not open up and satisfy him as well?

Best of luck and pleasure!

ONLY JOKING

Question: How do men define a 50/50 relationship?

Answer: We cook/They eat; We suck/They fuck;
      We clean/They dirty.

What Kind of Black Man Do You Need?

Exploring nationality as a way to find the right sexual partner.

A Black man can be the most wonderful thing on the face of this earth. And he can be the worst. Unfortunately, many women don't know what they're getting in a Black man until they've already become involved with him, or found themselves laying in bed with him, wishing they were elsewhere. You need to know what you're getting before you go that far.

The cultural attitude of the country your man is from will be a big factor in the way he treats you and the way he makes love to you. In some countries, the men don't believe in giving women oral sex! Fuck that! If you're like most Sisters, you aint havin' no Brother that don't go "Down South"! What if your man won't let you get on top? His ass would hafta be be outta there! Where a Black man comes from will often determine whether or not he'll be a good lover.

So, before you consider getting involved with a man, take his background into consideration. Where does he come from? What's his religion? What is his native culture like? Do they have any hang-ups or unusual customs in his country? Because nationality often plays an important role in a man's personality and his sexual attitude, we shall now explore aspects of Black men from different places.

American Black Men

Usually a mixture of Native American, African and

European, these Black men come in a range of tones and shades. Many of them are tall. Their facial features vary. American Black men can slam! No doubt about it. When it comes to "hittin' the back", American Black men know what they're doing (unless they have a small prick and then they'll irritate you by poking you senselessly). They can usually do it several times and love to explore different positions. They don't get bored unless the women they're with are boring.

American Black men can be very sexy but will sometimes lack *sensuality*. The reason is this: they have really hard dicks, but they're sometimes too quick to stick them in you. Sure, they like foreplay, but they want the main course as soon as possible. They figure if they suck your nipples for a while and give you a little oral sex, you should be satisfied. Some American Black men don't realize a woman often needs more time to get ready. Many of them do not explore sensual massage or kissing other parts of the body such as the back, ankles, hands or feet. Maybe they think it's beneath them.

Older Black American men, especially some of those from the South, will scratch the hair on their chests and suck their teeth noisily after they make love to you. The ones without class will even scratch or tug at their balls. Some are tender and others become indifferent after they've had their fill.

Some American Black men are stuck in a cultural gap because they don't identify with any one country. They're African when it's convenient, American when it suits them and ass-kissers when it comes to dealing with White people. They also have unrealistic expectations of their women. They're sometimes too caught up in silicone fantasies and don't appreciate a real woman with real feelings. They're into fluff.

American Black men generally love to suck titties. Many of them are "Tit Worshipers" and are into a European standard of beauty. Some of them would like for you to put your finger in their anus but will deny it because they don't want you to think they're gay. Others fantasize about anal sex but will deny that also. Because a number of them have not traveled around the world or learned a second language, they think their way is the only way. For this reason, certain American Black men have limited scope. A percentage of them are cheap.

Caution: Some American Black men will try and stick it in your butt while doing it doggie-style. When you get pissed off, they'll say it was an accident. That's bull. If you're not with that back door action and your man tries it on the sneak tip, let him know you're not havin' it.

Potential Positive side effects: Powerful sexually, sensible, and cool. They are trendsetters and often imitated.

Potential Negative side effects: Narrow minded, conceited and ignorant. Robot factor: Moderate to heavy.

African Black men

Usually dark skinned with full features, African men love to fuck. Depending on what country they're from, they will speak English, French, Dutch, or their native dialect. They can be difficult for American women to understand.

Although they're always chasing after pussy, African men are more interested in the women that give them a hard time. They're family oriented and responsible with children. Some of them think American women are sluts. Because it is culturally acceptable for a man to marry several women in Africa, African men are rarely satisfied with one woman. Therefore, the less you give it up to them, the better. They like when you make them beg, because it makes sex a challenge. Kissing is not their specialty, though pleasant, but they will try to make up for it in other ways. Sometimes, those ways really count.

According to some American women, African men are direct in their lovemaking approach and can even be rough. On the other hand, some can be very sensual. The ones who aren't sensual won't care as much about pleasing you. They'll bone you until *they're* satisfied, turn over and go to sleep. If they have some genuine feeling for you, they may be kind enough to pat you on your backside before they roll over.

In certain parts of Africa, women were traditionally given what is called a "female circumcision" (their clitorises were sliced off when they reached puberty). Many women died from the operation. The ones that survived found they could no longer enjoy sex (the clitoris is what enables you to have an orgasm). This destruction of a woman's sexual pleasure was by design because in those cultures, women were not supposed to enjoy sex: a woman's sole sexual purpose was to bear her husband's children. Female circumcisions have been outlawed almost everywhere, but some African villages still adhere secretly to the tradition. Ironically, the old and respected African women in the villages are the ones to firmly uphold it!

African men routinely have dicks that are long and slim or long and meaty. They have a lot of power behind the thrust and can stay hard for a considerable amount of time. If they're feeling very frisky, they can really shake things around in there. Some American women say African men love to receive fellatio, but do not concern themselves with eating a woman's coochie. They supposedly haven't mastered the art of oral sex and don't plan to. According to these women, if you need a man to go down on you in order to reach your climax, don't look for an African man. You may or may not get lucky.

Some African men do not exercise enough. When young they may be fit, but they'll gain weight later. After a while, they can become really spoiled and won't last as long in bed. They'll expect you to do most of the work. If your African man ever becomes lazy, you'll get considerable practice on top.

Because some of them think "more is always better," they tend to wear too much cologne. Some of them dress well by American standards and some of them don't. Some don't lotion their skin often enough. Their feet are usually tough and crusty looking. The average African Black man is not cheap and will treat you like a queen, if he cares for you. The biggest complaint American women have is that they are extremely stubborn. They are also very macho and dense. **Caution:** Some African men have a plan. They'll say anything or screw anything American just to get a green card. **Positive side effects:** Generous, attentive and family oriented (polygamy is legal in many African countries). **Negative side effects:** Possessive, stubborn and very chauvinistic. Robot factor: Very intense.

West Indian Black men

Spicy and rich in culture, these men pride themselves on what they can do in bed. They are a mixture of Caribe Indian, African and European. They are also extremely horny. If they're from Jamaica, their features are often fine. Depending on what island they're from, some will look better than others. They're often hard workers and will have several jobs.

They will say anything to get into your panties and promise you the world. If they are not in love, they lose interest shortly after they get what they want. They usually know how to stroke a woman in all the right places. When making love, West Indian Black men talk a lot of shit. And they want you to constantly tell them how wonderful they are. They can be very gentlemanly, or they can treat you like trash. It depends on how they see you. If you want a good relationship with a West Indian man, you should wait as long as possible before you sleep with him. They can be generous if they have money.

West Indian men are also sly. They can say one thing and mean another. Some of them, particularly Jamaicans, are very competitive and have a "Royalty" complex. Even if they're dirt poor, they have to be the ruler. If a woman is more successful, smarter or popular than they are, they get turned off. Some, on the other hand will take money from a woman without a conscience. Never give them money! Take it instead!

Island men believe they're the best thing since sliced bread. Fortunately, most of them can back up that belief with action when they're "hittin' the skins." Like that bunny on T.V., they keep going and going! Their biggest fault is they can get so involved in *how* they're fucking you, they don't make sure you're really *enjoying* it. They forget that sometimes it takes more to satisfy a woman. They're infatuated with pussy and jealous of it at the same time. They often have contempt for a woman's menstrual cycle, but they do like strong coochie odor.

Although they always complain about "The White man", West Indian Black men somehow end up fantasizing about White women. They do not realize they have been brainwashed. Some of them know how to dress and others have trouble coordinating their colors. A lot of them wear suits that look like pajamas and some believe gold teeth look really sophisticated. Most of them like to wear tight underwear.

Caution: Some West Indian men really "eat" coochie. They have a tendency to bite.

Potential Positive side effects: Fun loving, smooth and long lasting in bed. They also make good Jerk chicken.

Potential Negative side effects: Unfaithful, arrogant and in love with guns. Robot factor: Intense

Latin Black men

Also spicy, these men are known to be good lovers. Caliente. Very hot. Because they revel in pleasures of the tongue, Latin men love to French kiss. They can spend half the night kissing you. They also eat a lot of garlic and pussy.

Latin Black men are a combination of Caribe Indian, Spanish European and African. Because of the nature of their culture, they can be extremely macho. They adore when you moan and whimper; "Ay Papi" while they're screwing you, because it makes them feel powerful. Some really know how to keep the variety going, others tend to be dense and unimaginative.

Latin Black men are into stroking fast and move with the excitement of Speedy Gonzales. They have a lot of energy, but some don't have enough stamina. They can pump well, but might burn themselves out before you reach your climax. They know they look sexy. This can make them lazy. Some prefer to lie on their backs and watch you bounce up and down and tell them how good *they* are. They also like to make love in positions that allow them to see your face. If you don't make a lot of noise when bedding a Latin Black man, he'll probably be disappointed. So, make a lot of noise. They also enjoy rubbing and caressing and calling you sexy names. They like drama.

Latin Black men love sex in the morning and on Sundays.

Some Hispanic men do not consider themselves Black even if their skin is darker than tar. The ones like this lack respect for Black women and will call you "Negrita" or hiss at you in the street like you're a dog or something. When dating you, they'll test your morality to see if you're what they consider to be a slut. Our suggestion: leave these types alone unless they've really proven themselves. Watch carefully for derogatory actions and comments and hold off sex for a long, long while.

Like African men, Latin Black men can wear too much funny-smelling cologne. Like West Indian men, they love under-garments that hug the cock. They usually dress suave, wearing pants that contour all the right places, nice shirts and attractive hairstyles. Older Latin Black men will wear white patent-leather shoes or some other item of clothing that looks wack and many of them will have visible panty lines.

Caution: Some Latin Black men have extremely high sperm counts and can get you pregnant just by looking at you.

Potential Positive side effects: Passionate, romantic and suave. Often adept at baseball.

Potential Negative side effects: Hot tempered, jealous and sometimes violent (some slap women, others prefer to punch). Most are very possessive. Robot factor: Intense.

Other

This includes Black men from different countries in Europe,
The Mid / Far East, Russia, Asia, East Asia and Australia.
Brothers from these places are rather difficult to categorize
because foreign cultures have influenced their sexuality. Some
of them will be good in bed and others will lack "The
Mandingo factor." Most of them will be into White women or
women of different races. In general, they are not racist or
prejudiced. They are often very liberal.

Some can look good because of their mixed nationalities.
Some may not be into brushing their teeth, or using deodorant.
They may be interesting in bed because they will differ from
other men you have slept with. They can also be very cheap.
If they speak an unusual language, they may be very pleasing
to the ear. However, the novelty of their uniqueness will wear
off, after which, you may find yourself bored. If they have
trouble speaking English, that presents a bigger problem. How
will you tell the man what you want? How will he know if he's
hitting the right spot? Depending on where they're from, some
foreign Brothers will not believe in women's rights and think a
gal's only purpose on this earth is to serve them. Check each
one out before you get with him. Robot factor: Will vary

👉 Keep in mind...

You'll never earn respect from any Black man unless you
demand it. If you want to be treated like a lady, you have to act
like one. A decent Black man deserves respect and the benefit
of the doubt, but some Brothers have no class and are used to
doing what they want with certain females. Respect *yourself*.

Once a Black man gets the idea he can disrespect you, he'll
develop the habit of doing so very quickly. Like a robot, he'll
assimilate it into his programming and keep it there forever.
Let him know you're not the one to try it with. ❖

From His Mama's Nipple

To Yours: Is your man latched on correctly?

Once a mama's boy, always a mama's boy. Remember that. From the moment a male infant first places his mouth on his mother's nipple, he is beginning a pattern that will last his entire lifetime. He will stay locked onto his mother's nipple until he can get a hold of yours. After that, he'll go through life with his mouth full. You ask yourself: why are some Black men like babies?

A Mother's Mistake

Although certain women will not want to hear this, the truth has to be stated. **Certain Black mothers are the reason certain Black men never grow up! Because of these women, certain Black men remain emotional babies!**

Here, the blame must be properly placed. Unfortunately, a number of Black mothers encourage the same irresponsible behavior in their sons that they can't stand from their own husbands. These women allow their sons to live at home until they are well into their twenties and thirties and some don't want their sons to ever leave. These women do not realize they are creating monsters. When the sons are growing up, the mothers treat them differently from the daughters by failing to encourage responsibility and self-sufficiency in the home. The average boy is not required to wash dishes or do laundry, clean up after his siblings or cook. Yet, the female children in the family are required to do all of these things and more.

When a man is raised this way, he doesn't appreciate having

a woman. He approaches relationships with the attitude that the main function of a woman is to serve him. When he eventually leaves the nest, he searches for another home attendant to replace his mother. Any woman living with a man that does not know how to pick up after himself or help out around the house is essentially a live-in maid. If you have ever been with a man like this, you've probably experienced a great deal of frustration and upset, felt neglected and wanted to hit him over the head with a frying pan. What you should be doing is cursing out his mother because she is largely responsible. She's set the stage and he's playing the role.

One of the women we interviewed is married to a man that does absolutely nothing around the house. The husband works, but the wife has both a full time job and another job on evenings and Saturdays. The woman takes the daughter to school in the morning, works, comes home at 9:30pm and still has to cook and clean. She sleeps an average four hours a night. If for some reason she's late, her man will sit and wait for her to get home so that he can eat. If there are leftovers, he doesn't attempt to heat them up. He has no idea of how to use the microwave. He can't even make concentrated juice!

We asked the woman what her mother-in-law was like. As we suspected, the husband grew up with a mother who did everything for him. He never even boiled water. He was completely spoiled.

When speaking to the woman, the interviewer asked her what she sees in the man. The woman's response; "He's really a good man. He's not as bad as he seems."

Oh? After careful consideration, we've concluded the man must have a solid gold prick and/or a tongue that never stops licking. That's the only way we can see her putting up with him. What do you think?

Ask yourself: How hard should you have to work in order to be with a man? How hard should he work for you?

Dealing with the mama's boy

If you've figured out you are involved with a mama's boy, the first thing you'll have to realize and accept is he'll *always* be a mama's boy until the day one of them dies. Once a mama's boy, always a mama's boy. Nevertheless, there *are* ways to make life with this man easier.

Remember, men have to be trained.

Poorly trained men give you Hell. Properly trained men treat you wonderfully. For more information on training your man, see the chapters entitled: *Seven Easy steps* and *You are a Queen*. If, after reading these chapters training him with a "Stick" doesn't work, purchase the book: *Delilah Power* by Tannis Blackman, available through Swing Street Publishing. In this book, you will learn the techniques of "The Carrot Method". For purchasing information, contact Swing Street directly. See the order form at the end of this publication.

Remember, the method of treatment should be consistent with the problem.

If he insists on acting like a child, treat him like one. Punish him when he misbehaves and reward him when he does good. Do not reward negative behavior. For example, if he does something you don't like and you argue about it, don't become weakened by his silence or his anger. Do not turn around and do something nice to try and make up. You are sending him the message that it is okay for him to treat you poorly. And this is exactly what he'll do. It is a natural subconscious response.

Give him time to cool down and then approach life as usual. If he insists on continuing with the nonsense, wait him out. Men don't usually stay angry as long as women do. Sure, you want to get on with your life and would prefer to have things the way they should be, but you know what? That's exactly what he's banking on. He knows you want peace and he's going to try and make you compromise your principles in order to have it. Don't do it. After a while, he'll get tired of the nonsense and acknowledge he can't manipulate you that way. He'll have to come up with other ways. And he will. While he's preoccupied with those thoughts, you'll be getting ready for the next round.

When he starts acting like "Mama's little baby," don't get bent out of shape.

Ignore the behavior until it goes away. If he's having a temper tantrum, the worst things you can do are press him to talk to you or let him know his behavior is upsetting. That's precisely what he wants. Don't give him what he wants. Unfortunately, most men do not appreciate the things they obtain too easily, your emotions included. If a man believes you're an easy person to manipulate, he will not respect you.

Never try to compete with his mother.

If he's constantly comparing you to his mother, tell him the next time he wants some pussy, he should call his mother instead of you. Men will often try to aggravate women by comparing them to old girlfriends and their mothers. They know how much women hate it. Even if you want to punch him in the face, laugh off his comparisons. Never let him know it's bothering you. Remember he's the childish one for playing such a silly game. When he realizes this particular tactic isn't working, it won't be fun anymore. He'll reluctantly cut it out.

Unfortunately, there will always be some women who will continue to raise sons in ways that make dealing with them impossible. But now that you know why a man turns out to be a mama's boy, you have the arsenal to battle this widespread problem. Just stay strong and let him know you are not a Sister to be played with. He can't help but respect you. Once a man respects you, he'll be motivated to love you even more. He'll work harder to make you happy.

If you have a young son...

The first thing to do is decide if you want to raise your son into a man who is self-sufficient, emotionally well-adjusted and mature. Assuming you do, remember that special treatment never helps him. He needs to develop backbone. He needs to be encouraged to overcome challenges. He needs the necessary tools to help him become a good father and competent provider. Remember, he is the future.

Foster responsibility. Give him regular tasks and reward him when he completes them. For example, he could have the job of mopping the house on Saturdays, cleaning the bathroom or cooking dinner one day of the week. Let him work for his allowance. Compliment him on a job well done and avoid harsh criticism. If he does not do the job correctly, show him the way and let him try again. With each new effort, show your appreciation. Let him know that you trust him and teach him honesty and integrity. Show you have faith in him.

Encourage independence. Place him on an equal level with his sisters (if he has any) or any female family member that is of the same age. Do not assign "Tasks for boys" and "Tasks for girls." Show your son how to cook, do laundry, clean and take care of younger siblings. He'll need these skills in the real world. Let girls take out garbage and help fix things around the house. Encourage your son to make his own decisions and ask for his advice or input on family matters. Tell him his opinion is important. When he sees that his feelings count, he will feel empowerered and want to do the right thing. He will also be more inclined to listen to you.

Teach him to respect Black women: Never allow your son to physically fight with his sisters. On the other hand, do not allow his sisters to speak to him disrespectfully. Avoid arguing with your husband or your man in front of your son. Never let your son see you involved in sex or a violent encounter with your man. This is traumatic for him and could ruin his view of women. He will not respect you. Never call your son terrible names or tell him he's stupid: you can do irreparable damage.

Teach him to respect his environment: Discourage your son (or daughter, for that matter) from littering, writing graffiti and urinating in the street. Teach him to respect animals. Keep a clean house. Show him the beauty of nature and encourage a reverence for all living things. Show him how to care.

Teach him to respect and be proud of himself: You don't have to be rich to be clean and neat. Teach your son proper hygiene and avoid giving him dirty clothes to wear. Keep his skin moisturized and show him how to clip his nails. Make sure he washes his body, brushes his teeth and combs his hair. Not only does this help him to have pride in his appearance, it also shows him that you care. He may fuss, but ultimately, he will love the attention. Black boys need monitoring and care for their physical and emotional development. If, as a mother, you don't give it to him, then who will?

Support him without treating him like a baby: Encourage him to achieve his goals. Show an interest in his interests. Help him with his homework. Take him with you to work one day and let him help you with a simple task. Let him see how hard you work for his sake. Make him understand and appreciate you as a mother and as a Black woman. Don't give him everything he wants. Always tell him how proud you are of him and give him "Tough love" when he deserves it. Be a *parent*, not a friend. Most of all, never, under any circumstances, let him get away with inappropriate behavior. ❖

Finding Mr. Right:
He is out there!

The information in this chapter is based upon the assumption you are looking for a steady relationship with a decent man, or you want to know if the relationship you have is a good one. By steady, we mean a relationship which involves monogamy since it is the safest kind of relationship in this day of AIDS. If you are not looking for a steady relationship, you may still find this chapter helpful in selecting men you want to date or sleep with. In any case, you should choose your men carefully.

Take the following mini-test to see just how much you know about finding a good man.

Sizing up a potential mate

1) When first meeting a man, you should tell him where you live.
a) True
b) False

2) What is the best way to meet a man?
a) Through friends and family or at work
b) In the street
c) Through a dating service
d) In a club
e) None of these ways are good

3) After meeting a man and having several phone conversations, it is okay to invite him to your home.
a) True
b) False

4) After meeting a man, it is a good idea to check out the information he gives you about himself.
a) Always
b) Usually
c) Sometimes
d) Never
e) I have never ever considered it.

5) A man that calls you a lot after he first meets you is more trustworthy.
a) True
b) False

6) As long as you use a condom, it isn't necessary to know a man's sexual history.
a) True
b) False

7) You can tell a man is carrying a disease if you look him over closely.
a) Always
b) Usually
c) Sometimes
d) Never
e) It doesn't make sense to look unless you're a doctor or a nurse.

8) A man's gestures and speech patterns can tell you if he's lying.
a) Always
b) Usually
c) Sometimes
d) Never
e) A man's gestures and speech have no connection with his being honest.

9) A mysterious man is more desirable than one who is honest and open.
a) True
b) False

10) In terms of Mr. Right, there is a man out there...
a) Who can fulfill your every need
b) Who may fulfill many of your needs but not all
c) Who can only fulfill some of your needs
d) That cannot fulfill most of your needs
e) Any man can fulfill all of your needs if he's trained properly and managed right.

11) Honesty in a new relationship is better than excitement.
a) True
b) False

12) There is no way to tell if a man is a bad seed.
a) True
b) False

*Scores for this test are posted at the end of the chapter and detailed results can be found at the end of this book.

What to really look for in a potential mate

The first thing you must do is decide what type of man you want and then pursue that type of man accordingly. For example, do you want a man that is a homebody or a man that loves night life? Do you like the athletic type? Is a man with a lot of money very attractive to you? Do you like sensitive men? What about the macho man? Some men are good for sex and nothing else. Any man can be of benefit to you, provided he is utilised for a specific purpose. The idea is to determine the purpose and then deal with the man according to what you want. And don't mix it up.

Does this sound like a cold approach to you? It really isn't. It's common sense. If you spend your life looking for Prince Charming, you will end up disappointed over and over again. A man is only a human being and will have a number of faults. He can't help it. The fact of the matter is this: romantic tales are fun as an escape, but they're not grounded in reality. If you want peace of mind, you have to accept the fact that no man will fulfill all of your needs. He may fulfill many, but he cannot fulfill all. This does not mean you should despair. It does mean you should pursue a man that fulfills as many of your needs as possible. In short, use your head.

One of the basic differences between most men and women is in the way the two sexes have traditionally approached their relationships. This is largely due to the roles men and women have played in society. Always subservient, women were taught to seek love before sex and to prefer the love of one man. Men on the other hand were afforded the luxury of fully exploring their sexuality. Women were conditioned to believe it was wrong to want sex when there was no love involved. Men on the other hand could have it all. Not anymore. All of that is changing. In some opinions, for the better.

Nowadays, the average Sister knows what time it is. She wants satisfaction and she wants it now. Go on, girl! Today, a Black woman is not going to settle for less. She wants a man that will please her and lift her up, not tear her down.

Unfortunately, many Black women are still guided by emotion and forget to listen to what their minds are telling them when they get involved with certain men. This is how they get caught up in lousy relationships. This is how they get taken advantage of.

In this chapter, we shall discuss ways to determine whether a man you're pursuing is a good choice or not. You'll know what qustions to ask and learn how to tune in to your intuitive "sixth sense". If, like most women, you're searching for Mr. Right, you'll know exactly where to look and what to look for. We will begin with what we call *Sign Language.*

Sign Language

"Sign Language" consists of non-verbal signs that are definite indications of a man's character. As you begin to sharpen your observational skills, you will be amazed at how clear these signs can be. When getting to know a new man, take careful note of the following:

The eyes. Watch his eyes. Do they focus directly on you, or do they avoid your own?

Eye contact is very important. A man who does not look you in the eye usually has something to hide.

When a man is lying, his eyes will glaze over slightly and his focus will shift. It happens quickly and the glaze disappears immediately, so you will have to watch closely. Unless that man has thoroughly prepared his lies in advance, he will most likely have the glaze. If a man you just met has the glaze, that man should be avoided.

Speech pattern. In this case, you must use your ears. Men who avoid showing you the glaze by not making eye contact will usually give themselves away with changes in their speech patterns. Listen carefully to what he's saying and how he's saying it. After speaking calmly for a while, does he suddenly begin to stutter? Does he suddenly lose his train of thought and fumble for words when you ask him questions like; "Why didn't you answer your pager all night?" or "Are you seeing someone else?" Or, does he suddenly become one-worded and give flat answers like "Yes." and "No." after he's already been talkative for a while? These things are all danger signs.

Body movement. Even if the man has successfully hidden

the glaze and can control his speech pattern, there is something else that will almost always give him away. His body. When a person is lying, the body goes through a number of physiological changes: the pulse quickens, sweat forms in several areas and there is a pervading feeling of discomfort. That discomfort can be mild to severe, depending on the seriousness of the particular lie. It is a normal human response.

The discomfort and other changes normally created in the body by lying are what a polygraph (lie detecting) machine picks up. A Black man telling a lie will begin to fidget, shift and look uncomfortable. He may giggle for no reason, ask you; "Why are you looking at me like that?" and then his mood will suddenly change. He'll become angry. The purpose of this is to try and throw you off the track. If you ask a man a particular question and he seems uncomfortable before getting angry, he is almost certainly lying. Keep staring at him in silence to let him know he's not fooling you. Don't stop staring at him until he gets hot under the collar. Make him squirm.

Secrecy. Something else to watch out for. If a man you're interested in is secretive and does not give you much information about his life, it is not because he is private, it is because he has something to hide. What is he, a CIA agent? With AIDS lurking right outside your door, why would you want a man who's a mystery?

In addition, some women get killed because they happen to be in the wrong place at the wrong time with men whose real identities and lifestyles are a mystery. The men turn out to be gay or worse yet, on someone's hit list. Murderers don't like witnesses. So when *he* goes, *you* go. Is that what you want?

The more a man cares for you, the more he will want to include you in his life. If a man is determined to keep you separated from the intimate parts of his life, it is because he is hiding something and wants to manipulate you. If a man doesn't respect you enough to be honest with you, he is not worth your time. Let him know you think more of yourself than that. Get rid of him and find yourself a better man.

Strange vibrations. Now, you get to use your sixth sense. If something about the man doesn't seem right, something probably isn't. Ignore how good he looks and pay attention to the feeling he gives you. Is he often pleasant but can make you uncomfortable sometimes? Does he say things that seem a little strange to you? Do you get invisible goose bumps on your neck or warning beeps in your head whenever you see him? There are a lot of crazy people in this world. The mental institutions are overcrowded and forced to create a bigger outpatient list. Result: more psychos. Pay close attention to:

Too much calling. If a man you just met calls you several times a day, that's not romantic, that's scary. He's probably obsessive. A man should show genuine interest in you without trying to monopolize every free moment you have.

Telescoping. Does he seem to watch your every move? When you go out together, does he seem fixed on what you're doing? When you make eye contact with other men, does he comment or stare at you with some hostility? Watch out for a man that does this. He's extremely jealous and a control freak. He's capable of violence.

Stalking. Does the man show up uninvited at your home, workplace, or elsewhere? Is he often waiting outside for you when you leave the house even though you weren't expecting him? Does he call you often and hang up on you? If he does any of these things, he could be extremely immature or he could be dangerous. Why chance it? Advice: Don't let him get too close to you. The closer he gets, the worse he'll get.

Inappropriate prying. Does he ask you questions that are none of his business? Does he want to know exactly where you are every minute of the day and insist you tell him your every thought? Does he get angry if you refuse to tell him everything he wants to know? Be wary if he does. He may have serious problems.

If you pay attention to what your intuition is telling you,

you will know when a man should be avoided. Learn to trust your instincts. They could save your life.

Pagers: Toys for some self-important Black men.

Many Black men need to feel important. That is why a number of them get pagers. If the only number a man gives you is for a pager, it is because he is involved with someone. Don't think for one moment he will be treating you any better than he is treating his wife or steady girlfriend. He's probably telling her he loves her and she's the only woman in his life. If he can lie to her like that, imagine what he'll do to you.

One woman we interviewed had a baby from a man whose only contact number was a pager. She gave him the keys to her apartment and she didn't even know where he lived. He happily strolled in and out of her life until she saw him in a bar with another woman one day. As it turned out, the man had two other kids from two other females at approximately the same time the woman we interviewed had hers. And he was living with still another woman! None of the women knew about the others and were in precisely the same situation (having a pager number and nothing else, giving him free and total access to their apartments, feeling frustrated, etc). The woman we interviewed loved the man and was totally devastated when he finally married yet another girl.

If a man can't give you his home number, he's playing games with you. If that's the case and you still want to deal with him, play the game to win. Deal with him this way: get what you can from him and leave your heart out of it. Take his money, have sex with him when you need it and leave him alone. Bottom line. A man like that isn't worth anything more. You might keep another man on the side, too. For more information on getting sex and money from a man, read *Delilah Power*.

Where is he from and what is he about?

As we've said in previous chapters, you need to know where

your man comes from and think about what that means. Consider the following true story: an American woman who married a man from Iraq went to his country for a short vacation and found herself a virtual prisoner there. She had no rights, was forced to stay with her husband's family and was told she could never return to the United States or ever speak to her own family again. Nobody cared that she was American. In Iraq, women are property. Her husband began to beat her and she found out she would be killed if she was caught trying to escape. It took several years before she found the opportunity to sneak out of the country and return to America. She literally risked her life just to get home.

That woman made a fatal mistake: she ignored the fact that her man was a Fundamentalist Muslim and put herself at risk by going to his country. When you are in love with a man, you will tend to trust him. But, no matter how much in love you are, you cannot change the person that he is. A man's ethnic background or nationality often makes him what he is.

What to look for

Availability. The man should be accessible to you whenever you want him. You should have a general idea of where he is at all times and be able to reach him if necessary.

Genuine interest. You should not have to chase him down in order to spend time with him. Let him pursue you. He should be eager to see you, willing to make time for you and ready to bring you into his life. He should make gestures to show you that he cares. Although flowers, cards and candy are not important to many Black men, they all know how important those things are to women. If he's interested in you, he'll go out of his way to please you. After all, you're worth it.

Honesty. This should probably be your greatest concern. Don't accept the "I don't want to talk about it." line when you ask him a question. He should be very willing to answer your questions and show integrity when dealing with you. If it seems you've chosen a poor time to ask, respect his feelings for the moment and approach him later, possibly in a different way, but make sure he eventually answers you. If he never satisfies your need to know, he may be a "Get over artist." Observe how he deals with other people. If he's a "Get over artist" in other areas of his life, you can believe he's ready to "get over" on you.

Emotional Readiness. If the man you're interested in uses foul language when speaking of his ex-girlfriends or seems to get angry about things his ex-girlfriend is currently doing, he's still attached to the woman. He is not ready to get involved with you. He may think he is, but he's not.

How a man talks about his ex-girlfriends can tell you a lot about his personality. If he's mature, he'll tell you things didn't work out between them and leave it at that. If he always calls the woman a bitch and badmouths her, he's childish or unwilling to accept his half of the blame for what happened. Remember, there's always two sides to every story. If the ex-girlfriend could tell you her side, you would probably be shocked by the things he did. In addition, he'll have worse to say about you if your own relationship doesn't work out.

If you are careful in selecting the men you date, you have a much better chance of establishing a good relationship. If you ignore the warning signs, allow men to manipulate you and fail to ask questions, you are headed for misery. The choice is up to you!

Finding Mr. Right
Test Scores

On the following page are scores for your answers. Add the score numbers and check the total against the results at the back of this book. You may be surprised by what you learn.

Question 1	**Score**	**Question 8**	**Score**
A	0	A	3
B	5	B	5
		C	4
Question 2		D	2
A	5	E	1
B	2		
C	4	**Question 9**	
D	3	A	0
E	1	B	5

Question 3	**Score**	**Question 10**	
A	0	A	2
B	5	B	5
		C	4
Question 4		D	3
A	5	E	1
B	4		
C	3	**Question 11**	
D	2	A	5
E	1	B	0

Question 5	**Score**	**Question 12**	
A	0	A	0
B	5	B	5

Question 6

A	0
B	5

* On page 149, you will find a detailed explanation of the score for each answer you have chosen. Once you have totaled your answers, turn to page 150 for a complete and comprehensive evaluation of your total score.

Question 7

A	2
B	3
C	5
D	1
E	0

ONLY JOKING

Question: What did God say after He created Man?

Answer: "I can do better than this."

The Real Culprit

Why the Black man is responsible for the breakdown of the family.

All around us, Black families are falling apart and there seems to be little anyone can do about it. In fact, divorce and separation is practically encouraged nowadays. In a society where gay life is considered "En Vogue," it becomes even more difficult to maintain a solid relationship with a member of the opposite sex. While some sisters can and should be held accountable for a number of the problems Black families are having, it is the Black man who has caused the greatest strife. There is a saying: When a man and a woman have a baby, that baby is *half* his and *all* hers. This is how many Black men view having children. This is why it is so easy for some of them to walk away and leave their families with little or no conscience, why so many Black women find themselves raising their children alone.

Being of greater physical strength, the African-American male has traditionally dominated the Black woman, thus causing her a considerable amount of psychological, physical and emotional harm. Although many Black women today are enjoying their independence, some sisters find themselves continually being oppressed by their men and treated poorly. While the law supposedly provides protection for women, it is still very common for jealous, possessive men to kill them. How many women do you know that are physically capable of abusing a man? When a Black man is angry, he can find the perfect outlet in the weaker sex. Thus, many Black children have been the unfortunate observers of domestic abuse. This has further served to destroy the family unit.

How many of you Sisters reading this book have a deep, dark

secret, a secret you've been keeping since you were a child, a secret involving an adult male family member? Some Black men, the scum of the earth, have ruined their families by engaging in incest with one or more of the young females. This is a disgrace, yet so many men do it and get away with it. This is one of the main reasons why many young girls run away from home or grow up to be prostitutes, battered women or worse. This is the reality many young women have to face. How can a family unit thrive when a man is behaving in this manner?

AN HISTORICAL PERSPECTIVE

Because the present is a product of the past, we shall explore historical aspects that will illustrate, without question, why the Black man is "The real culprit" and responsible for the complete breakdown of the Black family.

During the days of slavery, a Black woman belonged first to her White master and then to her Black husband. After she served the White man, she was then required to serve the Black one. Even after her indentured service was finished for the day, a long work day totaling sixteen hours or more, she still had to deal with her Black man's problems and she suffered abuse at his hands. The frustration he felt was thrust upon her through physical violence and emotional torment.

In 1870, Black men obtained the right to vote. This was fifty years before any woman, white or black was allowed to vote in 1920. This means that for many years, Black men had more say in Government policies and more power to change their positions than did Black women or White women for that matter. In addition, the man has traditionally been the head of the household. Therefore, the Black man has historically been in control of the destiny of his woman and his family. It is therefore his fault that the family unit has broken down.

This is illustrated today by the fact that children from families containing a strong father figure tend to be more productive and less inclined to engage in destructive activities. One woman we interviewed, an educator with a P.H.D in Education and a B.A. in Psychology, agreed to share some of her observations from many years of teaching adolescents.

"During the course of the school year, it becomes easy to determine which students come from a balanced household and which do not. While many single-mother households produce well adjusted children, I have noticed a distinct difference between those students that have a positive male role model in the household, particularly a father, and those that do not. In addition, many of the young Black boys in the classroom who do not have a father at home grow up with the notion that it is okay for a man to make babies and not be an integral part of their lives. They see how wretched some of their own fathers are and later find themselves destined to repeat the same behavior."

It is a vicious cycle. If a Black man produces a son and does not nurture that son, the son will grow up to be a father who produces a son he does not nurture and so on.

Below are the results of portions of a nationwide survey we conducted. We randomly chose African-American women of various economic levels. All of the women have children. Some are married, some are divorced and some have always been single parents. We gave them a questionnaire and asked them to complete it as honestly as possible. The results we obtained are very disturbing.

1] How often does your child/children see their father?

Everyday: 22%

2-3 times a week: 17%

Once a week: 12%

2-3 times a month: 19%

Once a month or less often: 30%

2] Does the children's father make it his business to attend
school meetings for the children and/or become acquainted
with the children's educators?

Always: 24%

Often: 6%

Sometimes: 29%

Never: 41%

3] Does your children's father provide adequate financial
support?

Yes: 33%

No: 58%

Undecided: 9%

4] How often does the father of your children provide time for
quality interaction and/or plan special events that the children
will enjoy?

Always: 13%

Often: 18%

Sometimes: 34%

Rarcly: 19%

Never: 16%

5] If the children's father lives with you, does he handle equal responsibility at home with the children?

Yes: 24%

No: 66%

Undecided: 10%

6] Who usually cooks for the entire family?

Mother: 63%

Father: 18%

Other: 19%

7] In the event of an an emergency, can you contact the children's father?

Yes: 51%

No: 49%

8] Do you suspect your children's father is having an affair or has had affairs during the time you were together?

Yes: 43%

No: 17%

Don't know: 40%

9] Does or did your children's father treat you the way you feel/felt you should be/have been treated? In other words, is or was he beneficial to your self esteem?

Yes: 47%

No: 36%

Unsure: 17%

10] Overall, do you feel your children's father is a decent man?

Yes: 46%

No: 47%

Undecided: 7%

The results speak for themselves.

There was a time when the average Black man would open doors for you, take your coat and speak to you with the utmost respect. The average Black man was polite, well-mannered and thoughtful. Black men weren't writing songs that degraded Black women by calling them "Bitches" and "Whores" and they weren't gang-raping and they weren't pulling out guns every chance they got. Black men weren't pissing in the street in front of children, writing all over their buildings and ruining their neighborhoods with drugs and murder. In the days back when, the average Black man was a real man, no matter how bad his situation was, a Black man still had some pride in himself and his people.

Nowadays, things are different and it's terrifying. Look around and you see so many of our men in jail, on drugs, acting gay, being bums, chasing White girls, selling drugs, trying to be rappers, trying to be gangsters and acting just plain stupid. Finding a decent brother to date or marry is hard.

These men have no character and are very quick to blame somebody else for their problems. What they need to do is take a good look at themselves. But, they won't do that. Instead, they'll passionately moan and holler; "The White man is responsible for everything. It's a conspiracy!"

BLACK MEN LOVE TO BLAME "THE WHITE MAN" FOR EVERYTHING!

Did "The White man" force those rappers to write songs that degrade Black women? Does "The White man" force Black men to idolize those rappers and play their music?

There are no other men on the face of this earth, no men of any other race, creed or color who write and listen to songs that degrade their women, knowing the songs are played worldwide. Only Black men do that.

Should they wonder then, why people at home and from other countries often view them so poorly? Whose fault is it, really?

What about the way Black men are killing each other? Look at what's happening to some our prominent Rap artists. Popular artists have been gunned down in cold blood by so-called "Brothers". Does "The White man" put a gun in the hands of every Black man that goes out there and kills his own brothers? The answer is no. Granted, White America is giving us some problems, but there are more opportunities for Black people than ever before. Black men who blame "The White man" have no one to blame but themselves. In addition, any celebrity who promotes violence against his own through music is irresponsible and setting the stage for his own demise. Like it or not, when you become a public figure, you also become a role model and gain the power to shape young minds. If you abuse that power, you don't deserve respect.

Why is it then, that so many Black men fail to live up to their responsibilities and their heritage? This question shall be answered in the chapter entitled; "The Sucker Syndrome". ❋

ONLY JOKING

Question: How are men like noodles?

Answer: They're always in hot water, they have no taste and they never have enough dough.

Penises and Personalities:
Learning a Black man's hidden secrets by studying his private parts.

Penistry: An historical perspective

In ancient times, women were often forced to marry men they hardly knew. Because of her subservient position in society, a young woman would find herself living, eating, sleeping and making love with a man whose tastes, habits and experiences were unknown to her. This has spelled disaster for many innocent females. In a number of foreign countries today, new brides that are not pleasing to their husbands die mysteriously, disappear and worse. It is therefore a matter of *life or death* for some women to learn their men as quickly as possible to avoid upsetting them and meeting with terrible fates. If these women could know what you are about to learn, they would have a better chance at a happy life.

Over the centuries, many studies have been done to determine how a person's physical attributes affect his or her personality. Does the shape of a person's eyes or the bumps on his head mean anything? Many experts think so. In an attempt to understand personalities better, the art of palm reading, face reading, gestures and psychology have all been explored and developed. Sometimes, to no avail.

Unfortunately, until now, few women have ventured to the depth of a man's physical being and the one place he nurtures and cherishes as his own soul in order to find the truth. His penis. It is our belief, based on our extensive research, that a man's penis holds many answers the palm, the face and gestures do not. Why do you think men are so protective of their penises? They're afraid to be found out. If you know what to look for, you can make an accurate assessment of a man's personality after just one sexual encounter. Doesn't that sound exciting?

Until now, few women have had this advantage. Few women were briefed in the art of Penistry. We are about to teach it to you. In this chapter you will learn what you need to know to analyze your Black man and use this knowledge to make your relationships more fulfilling. You will be able to spot potential problems in a man, take the necessary steps to correct them and know when it's time to get rid of him altogether. Pay close attention and **BEWARE**: The information you are about to receive is powerful and will give you a clear edge over your man. Please use but don't abuse your new power.

GETTING READY

Okay. Let's assume he's there in front of you and you're ready to begin your evaluation. Start by having him undress. You may use whatever seductive ploy you can think of to do this. Ask him to stand in front of you naked. He should be fully aroused and erect. Don't let him suspect that you are implementing the art of Penistry (if he finds out, he will most likely put his clothes on and leave). When he's totally relaxed and unsuspecting, then you can begin.

NOTE: A good time to do this is when you're about to perform oral sex on him. This way, you're already up close and personal.

YOUR NEXT MOVE

Determine the penis' angle as it protrudes from his abdomen. Is it pointing toward you, left or right, up or down?

Straight toward you: He is most likely a man that is direct and to the point. He is frank. He can also be a perfectionist.

Angled left: He may be subversive or the type of man that doesn't mean what he says or says what he means.

Angled right: He may be a downright liar, without a sense of humor, or a man that secretly believes in Communism.

Angled up: He's ambitious, usually optimistic and/or in high spirits. He may also be a man with an addictive personality. He may live life in the fast lane. He may run marathons.

Angled down: He's often a creature of habit and content wherever he is. He may also be prone to depression.

Then, examine each of the following:

Check the Color. Check to see if his meat has a healthy pallor. A Black man's penis should not look alien. The penis should have color that is close in shade to the rest of the man's body. For example: If you ever come across a light-skinned Brother with a dark-skinned dick or vise-versa, get out of there fast. He may be the devil.

Look for Fuzz on the Pole. Is the penis hairy? Do you find it scary? Beware! This uncommon creature is shifty and enjoys lurking in shadows. He may be a bouncer, a bartender, a retired tobacco industry worker or a unisex barber.

Check the Texture. Is it smooth or rough? Scaly or chafed?
Smooth: He takes good care of his penis.
Rough: He may have engaged in sex recently, either with his hand or with another woman.
Scaly/Chafed: He may masturbate frequently or have a skin condition. He may also be allergic to latex.

Check his balls. Are they loose? Tight? Are they very hairy?
Loose Balls: Older man and/or active sex life.
Tight Balls: Younger man, fast metabolism, diet high in protein, slow sex life.
Very hairy Balls: A robust taste for life or he has a rough approach with women.

Hairless Balls: He's either a coward or he may have incredible sexual stamina.

Extra-Long Balls: Most likely a philosopher. He may be an ordained, inter-faith minister.

AN UNUSUAL STORY

While researching in Santa Domingo, we learned of a very special man some of the people regarded as a prophet. His name was Cirilo and he was a striking man with black skin and teeth like bone. But, that wasn't the special part. Cirilo was born with *three testicles*. From childhood, he appeared to have uncanny psychic ability and a great deal of luck. As he grew older, his destiny was confirmed. People from all over the island would come to see him and ask for his blessing. To receive it, they would pay an amount of money and perform a small ritual. They would rub his bare testicles and say a prayer. Cirilo wore a robe and tailored pants with an open crotch that allowed his balls to hang freely. So many people came to see him, the lines outside of his makeshift church were incredible. Men, women and children wanting good luck waited patiently for their chance to meet "El hombre con las tres pelotitas." Although many of the people were poor, they spent what they could for the blessing. They recognized the power! And thanks to his gift, Cirilo was eventually able to move his family to a bigger house on the wealthier side of the island!

PENIS TYPES

We shall now explore the general types of penises most commonly seen by women. Please note that some men may possess a combination of two or more types of penises and should thus be evaluated accordingly. In addition, each penis type has varying degrees. This is only a basic guide. As each case is unique, use your own judgment and common sense.

THE BAT: This penis is usually long and stiff when stimulated. Its head and upper shaft are thick but the remainder becomes increasingly narrow to the base. It resembles a baseball bat. It creates unusual sensations within the vagina because of its adverse shape. Whether you will like it or not is anybody's guess. Black men with this type of penis tend to have moments when they are out of touch with reality and are often daydreamers who spend most of their time fantasizing about the things they'll never be able to do. They can also have a warped sense of humor. A man possessing "The Bat" can sometimes be overweight.

THE HOOK: The medical term for this penis is hyperspadius. It is classified by an abnormally curved organ with a small head. Although it is not too unpleasant to the eye, a penis like this can prevent orgasm because it stabs the vagina at weird angles. Amazingly, it can be as hard as a metal pole. A female in love will learn how to work with it. Black men with this type of penis tend to be users who don't mind living off of a woman in one way or another. They're very often unfaithful and will snare you with their lies. They also have a grandiose attitude and believe their lovemaking is much better than it really is. They do try their best to please you in bed. They're constantly motivated by ego. But, even if they don't hit the spot, you will probably give them a decent grade for effort. Men with "The Hook" are often skinny and some of them smoke cigars.

THE LEFT/RIGHT-HAND CURVE: Actually classified as Hyperspadius but not enough to turn you off, these penises can feel very pleasing to the woman that likes to wiggle. Weighty and dense, The Left/Right-hand Curve can go on thrusting for hours. It can open you up like a corkscrew. Black men with this penis are sometimes arrogant because they're used to making women moan, especially if what they have between the legs is large. They're often dark-skinned. They may expect you to bend & kiss their asses after they've made love to you.

Don't do it! If The Curve says you're the only woman in his life, he may mean it for the moment, but trust your own instincts. Play hard to get. Make him want you. Men between the heights of 5'10"- 6'3" often have this kind of penis.

THE LIGHT BULB: Although this penis only slightly resembles a light bulb, we have decided to use the name to create better imagery for our readers. This penis has a very large head in comparison to its shaft. The head looks almost like a knob. It's usually straight and smooth and has the effect of a battering ram inside the vagina. Black men with "The Light bulb" like to be in control and think making a woman scream in bed means pleasing her. Sometimes, it does. But because "The Light bulb" can become too rough, you must let him know when the pleasure stops and the pain begins. Men with this type of penis are usually stocky and macho. For some reason, their names are often Anthony or Fred.

THE CONE: Totally unlike any other dick you've had before, "The Cone" can be rather scary. Fat at the base and narrow at the tip, it looks like it's about to erupt. It can be long or short, thick or thin. It's never completely hard. Its owner can have just about any build and look any way you can imagine. Watch out for a man with this type of penis. Black men with "The Cone" are often sadistic and warped. Filled with anger, they have problems achieving orgasms and will thus impale you until you can't take it anymore. There's lava brewing in his balls, so try not to get burned. Cowards, bullies and psychotic boxers who bite are cursed with this penis. They'll have menacing hands and feet. Men with a really skinny version of The Cone have penises that look like a carrot. Go figure.

THE PHILLY BLUNT: Narrower at both tip and base and thick in the middle, this penis is another one to be wary of. It resembles a marijuana cigarette and is just as dangerous to your health. Its possessor can be resentful and spiteful. He can also be cowardly. He may be your local District Attorney. He's extremely possessive and will constantly imagine you are up to no good. He wants to prosecute everybody. He likes for you to sit on his face before penetration and will then make you do most or all of the sexual work on top. If the penis is long, he has a good sense of humor. If it is small, he has a bad temper and an inferiority complex. Black men with "The Philly Blunt" are often short. Some suffer from "The Napoleon Syndrome" and have a bald spot at the back of their heads.

THE TWO-TONE: Here's one we're sure a number of you have seen. Pink or beige at the tip with a brown or black shaft, this penis will definitely make you wonder. You ask yourself; "Why is his dick two colors when the rest of his body is one?" Answer: He's moody and unpredictable and likes to masturbate. Black men with two-tone penises can be both sweet and mean at the same time. They often have fat stomachs. If the sight of this penis does not turn you off, it can actually be pleasing when inside of you. "The Two-Tone" gets incredibly hard. One thing to watch out for: men that have "The Two-Tone" in combination with "The Hook, Cone or Blunt" can turn out to be schizophrenic, psychopathic or both. A number of Two-Tones like to play the drums.

THE BENDER: This penis is not curved, it's actually bent somewhere in the middle like a folded toilet paper roll. It can be bent in any direction. Although the vagina can conform to just about any shape, you wouldn't want it to conform to this. It doesn't feel normal. You will wonder how a penis such as this could even exist. Its owner will occasionally have a twisted sense of humor or suffer from periods of nervousness and stress. He can be timid or obsessive, indecisive or fixated. He may be a real weirdo. Black men with this type of penis often have some other physical oddity such as a staring eye or an extra finger. He may be from space. As there is a lot of talk about aliens nowadays, it is advisable to make sure he has a navel (otherwise, he was never born), and red blood. He might even be from England.

THE UPWARD SWING: Considered most normal, this penis feels wonderful because it strokes the cervix and walls in ways that will make you tingle. It leans away from his body and then gently curves up to the sky. Black men with "The Upward Swing" got it goin' on. Unfortunately, all the other women will think so too and he'll probably give you a lot of headache if you let him. He enjoys women. You have to stand your ground with this one. If his penis is big, you'll be ready to start worshiping him. If it's smaller, it will still hit spots that will make you come back for more. Men with "The Upward Swing" are fun to be with and know how to use their hands and lips. Astrologically, they are often fire and air signs. They are usually of medium build, muscular and healthy.

THE DRIP: This is an interesting penis because it is usually small. When stimulated, it becomes wetter than a pussy and will stay that way. If you are into "Dog Water" this is the ideal penis for you. Otherwise, the only way you can deal with it is if you truly love the man. "The Drip" is constantly leaking. Black men with this penis are often in touch with their feminine side and have soft voices. They're passive, generous and fall in love easily. They can be terrific liars. If your man has "The Drip," he will probably enjoy going down on you and will stay there for hours. Afterwards, if you choose not to let him penetrate you, he will pout and sulk, but he'll accept it. He knows his small penis is not all that satisfying. He may aspire to do social work and like to be around children. He'll be compassionate to both you and your pets if you have any. In fact, "The Drip" is really a nice guy. If you "diss" him too much though, he will vanish without a trace.

THE WORM: This penis is really scary. It's really long and skinny as a frank. You read it right. Sometimes jet black, it jumps and dives and ripples like the deepest ocean. Only a snake charmer can tame it. It will hypnotize you and put the fear of death in your heart. For some very bizarre reason, every Black man with a documented case of "The Worm" is a

Capricorn born under a #9 numerology year. Also, their names often begin with the letter "J." Sadly, a man who has The Worm is usually the nicest man you'd ever want to meet and genuinely good people. Is it enough to make you overlook the fact that he's not gifted? You decide.

THE KNOBBY: The name speaks for itself. This penis has a twisted appearance and is never completely hard. It can be big enough to get things going, but will loose power in the home stretch. Black men with "The Knobby" have similar personalities. They have trouble finishing projects. They are often kind men and will sometimes have money, but in terms of relationships, they rarely commit. They are often the keepers of important secrets and have trouble looking you in the eye. Sexually, they're mediocre. They don't kiss well and are rough with the hands. They don't really care if you go down on them or not. For them, sex is okay, but no big deal. They generally will do what you ask, but can be very stubborn. Older men and Libras will sometimes have this type of penis.

THE LIFELESS: If you ever come across a penis like this, head in the opposite direction. You will spend your life frustrated. If the Black man with "The Lifeless" has money, you'll find yourself trading happiness for material comforts. He can be a gentle man, a patient man and a decent man. He can also be perverted, malicious and deceitful. He knows his woman is bursting at the seams because she needs some solid thrusting. He'll try pleasing her with his tongue, but will always be very suspicious of her when she goes out late at night. Men with "The Lifeless" usually have a lackluster appearance. They slouch and mumble and have difficulty making eye contact. Former football players sometimes have "The Lifeless." Otherwise, men with "The Lifeless" are usually the average type and sometimes out of shape or have medical problems. Heavy drug and alcohol users are also candidates. If you're sure your man doesn't use drugs, get him to the doctor for a check-up. You might also buy him some yohimbine.

THE IDEAL: Smooth and sizable, hard and even, this is the penis every woman dreams about and never forgets if she ever has it. The man with "The Ideal" is a real lover, a stud that knows where to go, when to get there and when to come back. He can come in any shape or shade. He usually has sensuous lips, masculine hands and mad tight buttocks. He's confident, calm and patient. He can sustain an erection as long as you desire because he has the ultimate control. He is not a man to be trusted. He gets hard when the wind blows. If you like a challenge, stick around. He will give you one. He enjoys making women beg. Men with this type of penis are very proud of their endowment and want the whole female world to see what they have. Use a thick condom with this one.

In Conclusion...

If, like most women, you are on a quest for the near-perfect man, we suggest you begin your search in his pants. While no man is absolutely perfect, you will find the art of Penistry a tremendous aid in determining which man will be most perfect for you! Happy Trails and Bon Appetit!

ONLY JOKING

Question: What's twelve inches long and white?

Answer: Nothing.

The Sucker Syndrome

What makes a man a sucker?

Historically, there have always been undesirable types who devoted their lives to making women miserable. The Marquis de Sade for example, was a member of the French nobility who found great joy in torturing women while having sex with them and later killing them. And what about our wonderful United States, where women could not vote until only decades ago? *Men* were fully responsible for that. Women all over the world are battered and killed by possessive, jealous men. In some countries, women are forced to cover their faces whenever they go out in the street and others have their faces so badly scarred by their husbands as part of their culture, no one else would want to see them.

For many men, women are property, objects to be used, abused and discarded. How many times have you had this experience: a man passing by stared at your flesh so intently, you felt like a piece of meat? It's as if you have no brain, no feelings, nothing. When a man sizes you up like that, he's assessing your value like a rancher assesses the value of a cow. He wants so desperately to eat you, but once he's had his fill, he can walk away without a conscience and leave you feeling used. And as you all have seen, some men are too quick to seek out a woman much younger than they are, someone whose innocence they prey upon. Not all men are this way, but every woman reading this book has likely come across some. It can be very disheartening.

As far as certain men are concerned, they can never be wrong, someone else is always the cause of their problems and they are constantly looking for someone to replace their mothers. A man spends the first nine months of his life getting out of a pussy and the rest of his life trying to get back in. Why do some men care so little about a woman's feelings? In this chapter we will attempt to find out.

While any type of man can be a sucker, we have found that the Black men on the list are the worst kind. After hundreds of years of separation, you would think all Black men would devote their lives to keeping their families together, to making relationships work with their Black Queens and doing something to help their entire race. Some Black men do, and to those magnificent brothers we give props. The others however, are sorry examples of Black men and the ones we shall focus on in this chapter. If a Black man reads this chapter, or any portion of this book thereof, and that man becomes offended, it is likely because something he read applies to him and he knows it. The truth hurts. He also knows he's been busted.

We shall now begin with a description of those sorry motherfuckers that call themselves men. We have concluded that they are afflicted with a condition we call...

THE SUCKER SYNDROME

Black men who suffer from this deteriorating condition can exhibit symptoms ranging from low self esteem to lack of integrity and character. They can be dishonest, unprincipled and sleazy. They can also be downright wicked.

The following is a list of the various kinds you suckers you may encounter. Some are worse than others. The more items on the list that apply to the man, the bigger sucker he is. Keep in mind any Black man appearing on this list is one you have to watch. When you need him most, he'll fall off like a wet Band-Aid. Chances are he's got some issues and it's likely he'll be giving you major grief in the future.

TYPES OF SUCKERS

BLACK MEN who never admit they're wrong are **SUCKERS!** There has been considerable debate regarding this kind of sucker. Some experts feel it is a "man-thing" in general and has little to do with race. Others imply that it is learned behavior for certain males. We contend that some Black men in particular suffer from this condition and will blame their women for just about everything. The condition is very difficult to treat and incurable in most cases. Most of you will just have to live with it.

BLACK MEN who don't own up to their responsibilities are **SUCKERS!** A man like this has serious problems that can most likely be traced to childhood. This type of man does not want to grow up and rebels against authority. As we cannot function in any society without rules and responsibilities, this shiftless man is never completely happy. He flounces from woman to woman, job to job (or, no job at all), views commitment as a death sentence and has an excuse for everything. Sound familiar? If you are with a man like this, you have your hands full. While this condition is curable, it requires a great deal of work. You may be better off finding someone else.

BLACK MEN who abandon their children are **SUCKERS!** How many times have you heard a man tell you some girl he was seeing "got" pregnant as if he had nothing to do with it? How many men you know either don't see their children or refuse to provide support? The bottom line is this: If you have sex, you must be prepared for consequences such as pregnancy and disease. This applies to both men and women. If a man gets a woman pregnant it is the responsibility of both of them to provide for the child once it is here. A baby coming into the world is innocent. It didn't choose to come, it was brought here by the two people that had sex. If you are not prepared to deal with a baby, a disease or an abortion, the two of you should not be having sex.

BLACK MEN who are insensitive to the needs of their black women are **SUCKERS!** Many Black men don't realize that once the needs of the Black woman are met, she will do anything to make her man happy. Most Black women want to please. The insensitive man's condition is curable if the woman patiently works with him and refuses to accept anything less than she deserves. This does not mean she should be overly demanding. It does mean she should be firm about her position when her man misbehaves.

BLACK MEN who don't want to spend money on you are **SUCKERS!** Several of the women we interviewed had a mass of complaints about men like this and almost all have had an experience with a cheap man. If a man is interested in you he should be willing to invest the time, money and emotion in getting to know you and winning you for himself. One woman we interviewed spoke of a date she had with a man who reluctantly took her to the restaurant of her choice, an expensive one, and ordered onion rings for himself as a main course. She had lobster. After dinner, she ordered tea. She drank it and asked the waiter for another cup. Her date instructed the waiter to add more water to the old tea bag. Another man she dated took her to the beach and later to White Castle. While standing on line, he said; "Baby, I've figured out what I want. What are *you* planning to buy for yourself?"

BLACK MEN who take money from women when they themselves should have jobs are **SUCKERS!** A gold-digging Gigolo has no respect for himself or the woman he is taking money from. A gold-digging Gigolo has no respect for women in general. This type of behavior almost always goes back to childhood and a mother who did everything for him. This

usually attractive, but worthless type of Black man still lives at
home in his twenties or thirties because he doesn't have to pay
rent, wash his own clothes or cook dinner. His mommy does it
all. He's used to being served. He's never learned that a man
should stand on his own two feet and be the provider, not the
dependent. The gold-digging Gigolo is proud of his situation.
If a man has this condition, he will likely be dishonest as well,
using the hard-earned money his woman gives him to romance
some ho. Are you willing to finance this just to have him
around? This condition is incurable so if you have a man like
this, cut off his cash flow, give him an ultimatum and/or get rid
of him fast. He's a waste.

BLACK MEN with no ambition are **SUCKERS!** It's time to
stop blaming White America for all of our problems and take
responsibility for our lives! Any man that doesn't try to make a
better life for himself by getting out there and *working* for
what he wants doesn't deserve better! No one said it was going
to be easy...which leads us to our next syndrome sufferer...

BLACK MEN who sell drugs in their communities are
SUCKERS! So, he drives a fancy car and has a few dollars to
spend... at what price? Gunfights on street corners killing
innocent people, drive bys, whole families ruined, an increase
in AIDS, someone's daughter or sister behaving like a whore
and sons stealing from their own mothers for a five dollar
high? The black man who sells drugs is doing exactly what the
enemy wants him to do. The sad part is, he's too stupid to even
see it. He will also be involved with several women because
he has no regard for anyone except himself and could care less
if you love him or not. All he wants is to control you. Notice
how quick he is to stop calling you if you get on his nerves.
That's because in his mind, you're easily replaced. Next thing
you know, he's riding some ho around in his BMW and you're
beeping him twenty times and he's not calling you back. What

better word to describe this fool than *S-U-C-K-E-R?* What meaningful use could you possible have for this man?

BLACK MEN who have substance abuse problems are not necessarily **SUCKERS**, but they need help and can be **DANGEROUS!** Stay away from a man that has a drug problem. You can't trust him and you should be afraid of him. He will be capable of anything. When a person is under the influence of drugs, especially Crack, that person becomes someone else. That person does not care about you or have a conscience. That person will do whatever he or she has to do in order to get high. If you're involved with someone like this, you need to get out of the relationship. Don't believe anything a druggie says. He'll tell you he loves you one minute and he'll steal from you the next. He can also hurt you physically. Worse still, he's a high risk for a sexually transmitted disease.

BLACK MEN who knowingly chase after minors and have sex with them are **SUCKERS!** He is a low life and deserves to be castrated! That young girl is someone's daughter! What's the matter with him, can't he deal with a woman who is on his level chronologically and intellectually? The answer is NO! Any Black man that takes advantage of an underage girl in this way has got some serious problems. He's immature, has no morals and is a step short of brain dead. He needs to get punched in his face. These men have no respect for women in general and would just as soon have sex with their own mothers if they looked good enough. If you come across a man that leers at teenage girls while you're together, you've made a poor choice in a mate. Get rid of the bum!

BLACK MEN that engage in incest are worse than **SUCKERS!** They're **DEVIANT ASSHOLES!** In certain countries, it is very common for fathers to have sex with their daughters. It is an unspoken part of their male-dominated culture. One woman told us men in her country feel it is their right to take their daughter's virginity. Although everyone knows this, a girl who comes forth and accuses her father is called a liar and punished. With all the available pussy out there, why would a man choose to have sex with his own flesh and blood? They say a cookie is always better when you steal it. The taboo is what makes it exciting for them. Do they care about the emotional damage they're doing? Do they care that they're breaking the law? Not at all. Until they get caught, that is. Then they're hoping some big nigger in jail doesn't turn them into a girl!

BLACK MEN who only date White women are **SUCKERS!** This is one that really gets to us! With all the beautiful Sisters out there, why would any Black man need to go that way? What do White women have that we don't? Our research has given us some answers! We interviewed a large number of African-American men who say they only date White women. We asked for their most candid answers. The responses were truly enlightening. According to these men:

    • **The taboo and the novelty are exciting.** Both the Black man and White woman feel they shouldn't be doing it and that's exactly why they do. It's a rebellion against society. It's also something different. Any man will say a woman is a woman no matter the color, but each ethnic type has unique qualities. For some misguided Black men, having a White woman indicates success. Some pursue a White woman out of curiosity. None of the men we surveyed told us White women were better. But, some of them seemed to be using White women as an escape from their Blackness. They view White women as trophies. Others say they screw White women for revenge because White men have screwed Black women throughout slavery. Yea, sure. We contend these men are clearly burdened with self hatred. They're assholes. Period.

    • **There are a limited number of single Black women in their circles.** Some Black men claim they don't meet many

Black Women in their social circles or where they live. We would buy that if they were from a 1% Black population town like Salt Lake City, Utah. There are usually enough Black women to go around. If a Black man chooses to date a White woman with money rather than a hardworking Sister, he shouldn't be benefiting from The Emancipation Proclamation or Civil Rights Movement. In fact, he should still be a slave on a plantation somewhere saying; "Yes, Massuh." and living off fatback and hard-ass bread. He'd probably be perfectly happy kissing White ass for the rest of all eternity.

• **White women excuse their behavior.** One man we interviewed offered this insight; "So-called morally responsible White people (a.k.a. liberal White people and particularly White women) attribute a Black man's negative behavior to his inferior role in society and believe he is acting out his rage. This liberal White guilt causes them to *explain* rather than condemn negative behavior. When a White woman dates a black man and he treats her poorly, she rationalizes in this way and excuses it. He can therefore get away with murder." And some Black men do. One notable Black male, a man known for his preference for White women, has been quoted as saying; "If he's ever seen with a Black woman, it's because he's holding her for the police." He also says Black women do not have enough class for him. WHAT?!!! We believe this fool is in a state of denial and suffers not only from The Sucker Syndrome, but from a very deep form of self hatred as well. His mentality is scary. He's a real dick. In fact, he's a dick that needs to be castrated!

• **White women are more accommodating.** One Black man put it like this: "It's the Mandingo fantasy, don't you know? To a White woman, a Brother is a black sexual beast she wants to tame. To do this, she must shower him with kindness, meet his anger with benevolence, give him unlimited rein so that he can be free and thus return to her willingly. Bullshit. She just wants him to fuck her proper."

• **White women are more promiscuous a.k.a. "freaky"?** As one interview subject named "James" put it; "In my experience, the White women who become involved with Black men are much more likely to engage in anal sex, group sex, bestialism, etc. They're much freer about sex. Black men with special tastes find the perfect outlet in this type of woman." She has also been described as more submissive, thus making him feel powerful when in fact, he's a weak-willed little bitch. White women who fantasize about Black male potency are willing to try anything, according to the Brothers we surveyed. We interviewed several White women and were told Black men are better in bed hands down. These women can't get enough. Look around and you see they are invading our dating circles like roaches.

Truly despicable: Black men who prostitute themselves to White women. If you've ever been to the Caribbean, any part of the Caribbean, you've surely seen how the Black local men sell their bodies to White female tourists. We use the word "Sell," because, according to the locals, the White tourists essentially pay them to have sex. These women give the local men their hotel keys, buy them clothes and dinner, let them drive their rented cars and give them money. In return, the local men fuck them. Jamaica, Bahamas, Guadeloupe, Antigua, just about any tropical island is included.

A Black man who plays a part in this kind of prostitution has no character and is nothing more than a slave and an ass-kissing Uncle Tom. If he had any sense, he would know he is being used. To witness this is hurtful for a Black woman.

BLACK MEN who fool around on their wives and girlfriends are **SUCKERS!** In this age of HIV and AIDS, any man that puts his woman at risk by engaging in sex with another woman should be strung up by his balls and shot. Despite the risks, many men still choose to have unprotected sex with an unknown woman if she appears "Clean enough." Clean enough?!!! A woman one of our researchers knew from childhood contracted AIDS from her husband after several years of marriage and recently died, leaving behind a sickly, HIV infected infant.

BLACK MEN who physically or otherwise abuse their Black women are worse than **SUCKERS!** They're **PUNK BITCHES!** Any Black man that disrespects his Black Queen is a bully that probably got his ass kicked in school and/or by (a) family member(s) and feels a need to repeat the sadistic behavior as an adult. He remembers the humiliation he felt and believes it's time to get even. However, his aggression is always carefully directed at someone physically weaker than himself. He'll never try to abuse another man, because he knows he'll get his ass kicked again. If you have become involved with a man like this, seek assistance immediately! This man can only be healed with professional help and will end up hurting you or worse.

BISEXUAL BLACK MEN who do not inform their female partners of their sexual orientation are worse than **SUCKERS!** They're **MOTHERFUCKERS!** What worse thing for a woman, than to discover her man wears a dress during off hours, or spends his leisurely time "Giving buff jobs," "Riding The Hershey Highway," or bending over for "The Big One"? Do you want a man like that coming home to you? What about the increased risk of AIDS? Black men who hide their true sexuality from women deserve the worst punishment. Some people have written books to try and get us to "understand" and "tolerate" male homosexuality. Sorry. There's no understanding or feeling sympathy for a man who endangers your life by lying. We're sure you can relate. A woman has the right to know what kind of man she's having sex with. Man lies, woman dies. If in doubt, get the Hell out! Make it your mission to ask questions and investigate. Your life depends on it!

BLACK MEN who don't want to or don't know how to perform oral sex are **SUCKERS** because they're not sucking the right thing! EXAMPLE: You've gone down there, you've done your best and he seems satisfied. He lays back, tells you what a sweet mouth you have and instructs you to get on top. You frown and think: Wait! Aren't you forgetting something, Motherfucker? Where's your mouth motion, Son?

The sad truth is, many men do not know how to please a woman by going down on her and are too macho to admit it. Many of them refuse to take suggestions or be taught. They interpret a woman's requests as too demanding and a turn off. Have you ever been with a guy that actually ignored you when you told him to do something sexually or turned around and complained you were giving orders? One woman we interviewed spoke of a man she once dated who had a large gap between his front teeth. While performing oral sex on her, the man would suck her clitoris between the gap, wedging it and causing her excruciating pain. Although she cried out in agony, he insisted on doing it until one day she literally smacked his head away. Needless to say, she refused to let him go down on her after that. Through to the day they broke up, he never understood why she didn't like oral sex from him.

Note: Some men are really scared of coochie. They sincerely believe eating it can kill them. Others think they can sink their teeth into it like it's a hero sandwich or something.

BLACK MEN with small penises (who swear they've got footage) are **SUCKERS!** There's nothing wrong with having a small penis (yea, right). Still, a man with a small penis is not to blame for his "shortcomings." There are ways to make up for it if he's open and determined (and if you love him). Nevertheless, any man that makes false claims and/or thinks he can "Hit the Back" when he can't is suffering from The Sucker Syndrome and needs to get his act together.

> There are only two people in the world who will tell
> you penis size doesn't matter: a man with a small penis
> and a woman who has never had a big one.

Back to the issue of Suckers, here's something many Sisters feel should go high on the list...

BLACK MEN who make an issue of how a woman's feet look, when they themselves have the worst looking feet on the planet are **SUCKERS!!!** How dare some of these men complain about a woman's feet? Many Brothers have feet that belong in a horror movie and they don't even care! Some have crust and some have fungus. Many have toe jam. Others still, have rough skin and mad callouses. What makes them think a woman doesn't notice? If these men knew how much sexier they could be with a pedicure, they would make an emergency appointment with Dr. Scholl. Any Black man that can walk around on hooves and talk about a Black woman's feet is a bonafide **Sucker!!!**

As you can see, there are many ways a Black man can prove himself to be a sucker. Does he have any conscience about it? Can he change? Some suckers are happy just the way they are. **No one really knows what makes a Black man a sucker but there are several theories.** We shall now explore three of them in detail.

1] He was born that way. If that's the case, he'll always seek out women with low self-esteem for they are the only ones he can abuse. If it's an inbred part of his personality, he's a waste. A clear indication will be his constant resistance to change and improvement. You shouldn't have to tell him what to do. Any strong brother knows he's got to keep striving to make a better man out of himself. He's got to keep it real!

2] Experience has made him that way. If that's the case, why waste your time trying to correct what took years to happen? Why pay for something another woman did before you even got there? If you like to work for love, be our guest. You're better off looking for one of those Brothers from the Million Man March. At least some of those Brothers know what time it is. They need a decent Sister like yourself!

3] No one has ever taught him the right way. If this is the case, he still represents a lot of work, probably too much for it to be worth it. By the time he's a man, he thinks he knows it all already. There won't be much you can tell him. The only way he'll see his errors is if something major happens in his life like, a close brush with death or someone important to him dying. All of a sudden, he'll realize the terrible things he's been doing. Unfortunately, it's often too late. If you think your man is open to some lessons on true manhood, then get to it. We wish you the best of luck. You'll need it.

So, what's it gonna be?

Now that you are familiar with the different types of suckers, you are in a much better position to deal with your man. Keep in mind that no one is perfect, including you, and there will always be problems in relationships. What matters most is that there's communication, honesty and openness on both sides. If you can achieve those three things, you are well on your way to having a terrific relationship. Stick to your goal of better understanding and you will eventually get there! ❀

*" I don't wanna be
no Sucker. Woof."*

ONLY JOKING

Question: What is the difference between Government
         Bonds and men?

Answer: Government Bonds mature.

Sex with The Black Man

What you need to know to make it fantastic!

HIS TASTES

As some of you may have noticed, many Black men have specific tastes when it comes to women. First and foremost, Black men love Bootie. Big Butter booties. Round, firm booties. Wide, spread, you name it, they like it. They want them phat, but not flat. A brother can easily get lost in some good bootie. When allowed, the Black man will happily grab two handfuls of bootie and ride it until he's limp. That should take a long time. He loves to jiggle the flesh, slap it and make it vibrate. He loves to lift it up and spread it. From behind, he's in bootie heaven. He zeroes in like radar and zaps it!

The Black men we interviewed all conveyed a strong love of that area which juts out from behind a woman and is the last thing they see when she walks away. So what does that mean for a Sister?

She's in luck! Having been blessed with a shapely, prominent backside, the Black woman is in a good position. All she has to do is tempt the Black man she wants with that part of her body he can't resist. In short, the more she accentuates her butt, the crazier that Black man will get. Guaranteed.

Black men also love big, juicy thighs They want a woman they can really hold onto, a woman that feels like a woman. No anorexics. As a rule, they don't like overly muscular women either, but they do like a woman that takes care of her

body and is in good shape. A well-cared for body is a turn on.
Brothers want it firm to the touch, but yeilding to force.

How does a Black man make love?
If he's a real Black man, he makes love with a lot of gusto.
And he won't stop until the job is done. A real Black man
knows how to please his woman. When making love, he'll
work to control his orgasm until you're completely satisfied.
Having full, sensuous lips, he'll kiss you gently, nuzzle your
neck and slowly find his way to your breasts. When he begins
to suck on your nipples, you'll go wild!
If he's not afraid to go down on you, you're in for a treat.
When those juicy lips get a hold of you, you'll forget your
name. Brothers who know what they're doing use their
tongues in ways that should be against the law. A Black man
will lick you gently, explore every part of you and kiss you
between the thighs in ways that will make you scream.
Black men can also have an incredible amount of stamina.
They love to have sex, so they try to make it last as long as
possible. Some specialize in stroking and some are really good
at slamming. Depending on the size of the man, either can be
ideal. Each man is unique, but most fall into a certain category
as demonstrated in the chapter: *Who are you making love to.*
If you are lucky enough to have a Brother that can send the
shivers through your body, you need to do whatever necessary
to make him feel the same way. He deserves it. When you're
making love to a Black man, you need to think about...

KEEPING HIM HARD ALL NIGHT

Brothers we interviewed almost unanimously agreed they
were turned off by a woman that didn't work in bed. In other
words, a woman who just lays there and expects the man to do
it all is boring. The men also agreed that an overly aggressive

woman was another turn off. Where then, do you find the reasonable balance?

Instead of trying to perform for him, try to become tuned to what he is doing and respond to his body naturally.

Listen to his breathing. If he's laying there calmly and breathing normally, he's not as excited as he should be. If you do something that makes him gasp, you've got him. Keep at it. If you're working him over with your mouth and he holds onto your head, he's telling you not to move or stop. Don't.

Pay attention to his movements. If he's wiggling earnestly, he's probably having fun. If he's motionless, he's probably bored. Try and get him to wiggle.

Listen to what he tells you. Whenever he says he likes something you're doing, keep doing it. Explore that particular thing until he climaxes or becomes restless. If he's about to climax and you don't want him to, stop what you're doing and go on to something else. If he begins to get bored or restless, use some other move on him until his excitement builds again.

Ask him what he wants. Most men appreciate a considerate woman in bed, but many are afraid to say what they really want. If you can't draw information from him by asking straight out, ask him while you're in the process of actually doing something in bed. For example, if you're on top, making love to him, ask him if he likes a particular motion of your hips. Say; "Does this feel good? Do you like when I move around on it like this?" When he responds, ask him to tell you what he likes the best. When he tells you, do it.

Sexy Specifics

Seduce him with your eyes and mouth. The right stare can be an aphrodisiac. If you want to turn your man on this way, gaze up at him for a long moment. Make sure you have his direct attention. As he watches you, let your eyes drop and then lick your lips. Wait a few seconds before bringing your gaze back up. When you do, you'll see the lust in his eyes. **Seduce him with the way you walk and move.** Slow and confident are what makes a Black man's heart beat. When you have to bend over, don't do it with your legs spread. That's too obvious. Instead, put your knees together, poke your bootie in the air and reach for whatever it is you dropped. No Black man can resist watching. And getting excited. Remember what was said about booties at the beginning of this chapter. **Enticing clothing:** Wear something that will raise his blood pressure. Sleazy is great and so is teasing. Sometimes what a man can't see is the most exciting to him. Model lingerie that shows skin but covers the sexiest areas. Make him wonder what's underneath all the lace and satin. If you want to, you can either put it on or take it off in front of him. Some men really like to watch a woman dress and undress.

When making love...

From the front: He wants to feel like the master and will try to make you scream. Even if you don't feel like it, humor him and scream anyway. You can laugh about it to yourself when it's all over. Gently kiss and nibble on his chest if you can reach it. He'll go crazy.

From behind: Turn him on by arching your back and shaking your hair like a wild pony. Beg him to kill you with his incredible dick. Don't be shy. When he groans, grips your hips and starts smacking your butt-cheeks like a cowboy, you've got him where you want him. Make him ride that bad boy and see if he can stay on for more than ten seconds! (He'd better stay on for more than ten seconds!)

Suck on his fingers. No one knows exactly why, but Black men love it when you gently suck their fingers. Maybe they're imagining your mouth somewhere else. In any case, when you do it, make sure your mouth is really moist. Slide your lips as far down to the knuckle as possible. When you have the entire finger, suck it gently and let your tongue caress it. He'll lose his mortal mind. You can also lick the space between the fingers. The area is very sensitive and will make him shiver.

Use your hands and fingers on his back, shoulders, buttocks and waist. Don't dig your nails into him. Gently caress him as he strokes into you to urge him on.

Sensuous words: A man loves to know that he is pleasing the woman he is fucking. When you moan for him, you are telling him he is a real man. Few men have trouble responding to moans and coos. When he hears your heavy breathing in his ear and those whispers of encouragement, he will be motivated to work harder. You can also let him know when something he is doing is pleasing to you.

You can for example, say; "Baby, it feels so good when you do that." "I really love that." etc.

When he is doing something you don't particularly care for, you can tell him; "Honey, would you do _____ instead? I'd really love that." or, "That feels good. Now will you _____?"

This way you don't sound too demanding or critical.

Sexual Aids: Yohimbine and Red Stone are two well-known sexual enhancers. Check with your local health food store for more details. Some women have also had success giving their men Sea Moss drinks or Cayenne Pepper supplements. Ginseng tea has also been known to give a man an extra "rise."

Let him know how good he looks doing it. Most Black men are like this: If they could spend the entire evening watching themselves bang a woman out, they would do it. They're that big on themselves. Let your man know how masterful and unique he is and how fantastic he looks to you. Many Brothers are suckers for flattery. Say; "Boo, your body looks so good... those muscles!" or, "I love how you look on top of me.

It really turns me on." Tell him that and watch his reaction. Be nasty if you want: vulgarity has a place in bed and men love it.

IF YOU WANT TO PROLONG THE ACT...
Here is a technique that will give you the ultimate controlling edge over your horny man.

When you feel your man is about to ejaculate, grab his penis between your thumb and forefinger, at the base, just above his testicles. You'll feel a quivering beneath the surface. Pinch his penis *gently* between your two fingers and maintain a steady pressure. Doing this interrupts the flow of semen and forces it back. As you do this, whisper to your man that you don't want him to come yet. Tell him he has to keep pleasing you, because it feels too good for him to stop. Say it in a sexy way, not in a demanding way. Hold onto the penis until the quivering subsides. At that point, he'll be ready to keep going. And he'll perform! He'll realize *you* have the magic. Lastly...

Do whatever is within your power to please him

Unless he wants you to do something you find totally re-pulsive (like defecating on him or letting him piss on you– keep in mind some people actually like that), you should do your best to please him in bed. And unless he's a real asshole, all that work you're doing will motivate him to return the favor. It's a two way street. You might find yourself getting turned on by how excited he is. And when he knows he's turning you on, he'll get even more excited. If you find after a while that he's lazy, stop working overtime and tell him to get his act together. Try telling him nicely at first. If he doesn't respond, be firmer and if worse comes to worse, start a pussy boycott. Or, find somebody else. Do what you have to do. Who needs the headache?

Speaking of headaches, it's time to discuss another aspect of sex with the Black man, or better yet, an aspect that will amount to *no sex.* In this section, you will become good at:

RECOGNIZING SEXUAL PROBLEMS

Case #1: "The 60 second assassin."

Danielle met a man who seemed to be "The one." Arthur was attentive, considerate and generous. He was also very handsome. He didn't rush or pressure Danielle to do anything, he was the ultimate gentleman. When they finally wound up at Arthur's place, ready for action, Danielle knew it would be an incredible experience. It turned out to be incredibly awful! Arthur's gun was cocked and loaded, but it went off in less than a minute. Danielle tried several times on several occasions, with the same result. She couldn't believe it. The man of her dreams was a "60 second assassin"!

A "60 second assassin" might cause you to do something rash!

Danielle ended up having a string of sexually satisfying, but guilt-ridden affairs behind her man's back. If a man can't last long enough, his woman will never be happy.

Case #2: Competing with "Palmela," "Hanna" and "The Five Finger Discount."

Karen is living with a man she loves very much. She says he's thoughtful, takes great care of their two kids and seems devoted to her. The problem is, he doesn't want to make love to her anymore. No matter what she does, her man just isn't interested. While Karen doesn't suspect he's fooling around, she does wonder what's going on. She believes something is wrong with her and becomes both angry and withdrawn. After seeing several therapists, she realizes it isn't her problem, it's *his.* She considers going outside of the relationship for sex but knows she would feel guilty. It takes several frustrating years for her to find out her man is having a love affair with his hand! Palmela is destroying their relationship!

BLACK MEN LOVE TO JERK OFF!

Those are the cold, hard facts. No matter what your man tells you, you can bet he has a regular jerk-off schedule. If the average Black man could marry his hand rather than a woman, he probably would! While masturbation is usually healthy, some men can become hooked on it. It's an escape, they feel totally in control and they don't have to deal with a woman's demands. After a while, they can manage just fine without pussy. If your man isn't giving it to you the way he should be and he's not out there fooling around, he's probably infatuated with his own grip. How can you compete with that? He'll probably need some form of professional help in order to deal with his problem. He's an addict. Do you want to be sexually frustrated or do you want orgasms? Give him an ultimatum.

Case #3: Dealing with "The Dirty Dog."

Vanessa had almost the opposite problem of Karen. Her man *wouldn't stop* fucking her. He just wouldn't give her a rest. Every time Vanessa turned around, he was waving his dick at her, insisting they "get busy." When they first started dating, it was great. Vanessa felt sexy and wanted and desirable. Then after a while, it got boring. After all, she says, how many different ways can a man poke a woman? It seems her man was determined to find out. Vanessa likes sex and loved her man very much, but sometimes she felt like a piece of meat. She finally realized there was a problem when "regular sex" was no longer good enough and her man began asking her to do things she'd never even heard of. Vanessa had a man that was grossly oversexed.

SOME BLACK MEN HAVE DICKS THAT ARE MORE POWERFUL THAN THEIR BRAINS!!!

If those Black men could accomplish with their minds what they do with their dicks, they would probably rule the world!

If a man is oversexed, eventually he will tire of you. A sign that a man is oversexed is his determination to have sex with you no matter what the circumstances. The world could be ending and his last request would be a blow-job. He'll want to do it even if he's half-dead and he'll still do it if *you're* dead. That's pretty scary. Which brings us to the topic of...

Case #3: Scary Niggers.

There should be a whole chapter on this subject! A scary nigger is any Black man that looks weird, acts weird or does weird things in and out of bed. For example, one woman we interviewed spoke of a man she dated that took her out to dinner. While eating, he seemed to be staring at everything except her. The woman eventually asked her date why he wouldn't look at her. His response was; "I don't like to watch women eat." Scary.

Another woman dated a man that had to take a shower at 9:30pm every night. No matter where he was or what he was doing, he had to be home no later than 9:20pm so that he could be in the shower by 9:30pm. Do you know that man stopped making love to her one day and left so that he could go home and take a shower? She invited him to shower at her house but he refused. He could only shower in his own bathroom. Scary.

We recently heard a story about a man who believed he was a rooster in a former life. From what we understand, he would flap his wings and cluck like a chicken while having sex. Lord have mercy!

Another woman we interviewed slept with a man who was extremely handsome, but had feet that looked like hooves. Thick and crusty with sharp, twisted nails, they scratched her legs and broke skin during sex. The sex wasn't that bad, she said, but the feet made her very uneasy. They were really difficult to look at and they smelled funny. To top it off, he kept resting his feet on her and rubbing her with them every chance he got. And she actually put up with it! Now, that's what we call scary.

Do you have a story to tell about a scary nigger? Would you like to see it in print? If so, you may write to the following address. If your story is chosen, it will be included in an upcoming publication. You will be notified. You do not have to use your real name.

Send stories to:
Swing Street/NYIM
P.O. Box 846
Cathedral Station
215 West 104th Street
New York, N.Y. 10025-0846

GETTING WHAT YOU WANT AND NEED

Assuming you have a normal man, we will now discuss ways of enhancing the sexual experience with your man. While some brothers have a knack for pleasing a woman, there are others who need a little guidance. Sometimes, you literally have to "lead them by the nose." Following are a number of helpful suggestions.

Buy an erotic video and screen it before you let him watch it. When it gets to a part where the actor is doing something that looks really good to you, rub your man's thigh and say; "Ooh, I'd love for you to do that to me." If he forgets to do it when you're making love, say; "Ooh could you do that thing we talked about when we were watching the movie?" Smooth.

Buy a sex manual and leave it around the house when you know the two of you will be alone. A lot of Black men are nosy. And horny. If they see something spicy like that lying around, they'll pick it up. Put a bookmark in the part you really like. Or better yet, highlight things you like with a fluorescent highlight pen. If your man has half a brain, he'll begin to get ideas. Smooth.

Write him a sexy letter telling him about all your fantasies (fantasies you have about him, not another man) and all the things you would love for him to do to you. After he reads it, take the letter and read it to him. This is guaranteed to get him started. At that point, you can ask him to do what you wrote in the letter. Smooth.

If none of these tactics work, your man is denser than most and needs something intense to get him out of his stupor. For advice, you may write to *The Righteous Mother,* care of the address appearing earlier in this chapter. You should also purchase the book *Delilah Power,* by Tannis Blackman.

Delilah Power is available direct from Swing Street Publishing or at your local bookstore. See ordering form at the end of this book or contact Swing Street for more information.

WATCHING FOR DISEASE

When a woman is sexually active, disease will always be a major threat to her health and well-being. While no one likes to talk about sexually transmitted diseases, they are a reality in this day and age and need to be addressed. Nowadays, having sex can kill you. In this section, we will discuss different types of sexually transmitted diseases (STD's), how to identify them and the best ways to avoid getting them.

Acquired Immune Deficiency Syndrome (AIDS): Did you know that as a Black woman you are eighteen times more at risk of catching AIDS than just about anyone else? Scary, isn't it? The truth is, you take a much greater risk of getting AIDS than a man does when you have sex because it is easier for you as a woman to catch it. This is because you are receptive, or in other words, you are the one that receives/accepts the most bodily fluid (sperm). In many cases it only takes one sexual encounter for a woman to get the virus. A man usually has to have unprotected sex with an infected woman several times. Condoms are no guarantee, either. What if the condom breaks? AIDS kills by preventing the human body from protecting itself against disease. When the disease is in its advanced stages, something as simple as a common cold can be deadly. Most AIDS patients die of pneumonia. There are also various forms of Cancer linked to the disease, particularly one that causes lesions or sores in the skin. Numerous ailments are also caused by the medications used to treat AIDS. Although medical advancements have been promising in the fight against the disease, AIDS is currently incurable.

Although it is believed you cannot get AIDS from kissing, theoretically, if you have a sore in your mouth and you tongue kiss a guy who has AIDS, the virus can enter your body through the sore. The bottom line is, you can get it just about any way if you are intimately involved with a man. What then, should you do?

• Know the person you are going to have sex with very well before you get involved. Try to find out as much as you can about his background from other people. Does he have another girlfriend? Is he a player? Is he gay? If there's ever a question about his sexuality, stick to the old rule: when in doubt, throw it out. Is he usually with only one person? Is he looking to settle in with someone? Is he willing to take an AIDS test? All of these things are good to know.

• Always use a condom when having sex unless both you and your partner have taken an AIDS test. If you do choose to take the test and you both test negative, it is still a good idea to use a condom because he can always fool around later. Better safe than sorry. If he claims he's had the test done already and it was negative, don't take his word for it. Make him show you the paperwork. Explain it's nothing personal. You're better off hurting his feelings than ending up dead for believing a lie. If he's sincere, he should understand. Today, AIDS tests are available over-the-counter.

• Use alcohol and drugs in moderation because they can impair your judgment. If you use drugs or drink alcohol, you might do risky things because you're not in your clearest frame of mind and it's easier for someone to influence you. A lot of men still choose the risk of unprotected sex over using a condom and will do everything they can to convince you it's safe. When dating, stick to a two drink minimum and if you have to use drugs, go light on the other stimulants you use.

• Don't judge a book by its cover. Unless a man has full-blown AIDS, it is impossible to know he is infected. He can look perfectly healthy. There is no other way to know other than to have him tested. Many men refuse to be tested so your only other alternative is to protect yourself. Use condoms.

Herpes simplex 1 and 2: Incurable but not deadly, this STD is becoming an epidemic in the United States. Statistics show that as many as 1 in 5 White women have Herpes and the number is increasing for Black women. Herpes 1 is usually the cold sores you see on the mouth and Herpes 2 is usually on the sex organs, but the disease can occur anywhere on the body. When it appears on the arms, legs and chest of children, it is a form of the virus we call Varicella, or Chicken Pox. In adults, when it appears on the chest and stomach, it's called Shingles. Type 1&2 of the disease is characterized by small, blister-like eruptions on the mouth or genitals that occur periodically. The only way to tell if a man has Herpes is to examine his penis for the blisters and/or the resulting scar tissue. It is also possible to get Herpes if a man has a cold sore and he goes down on you. In addition, condoms may not always provide protection because the virus can leak over the rim. How to avoid it:

• Use a condom with spermicide. Studies have shown spermicides can act as a barrier against Herpes. Nonoxynol 9, the ingredient in spermicides, actually kills the virus.

• Examine your man's penis in the light before you

begin to play with it. If you see any strange bumps, scars or sores, question him about it and leave the sex alone until you know what's going on. If he can't give you an answer or he doesn't go to the doctor, he's probably hiding something. At this point, it's your choice to continue having sex with him or not. If you choose to continue, protect yourself with a condom.

• Avoid kissing a man with a cold sore or letting him use his mouth on your body. Remember, you can get Herpes anywhere on your body if there's a crack in the skin and that crack comes into contact with a cold sore or blister.

• Ask the man you are about to sleep with if he has the virus. Some people will not tell you at all and some will tell you if you ask. At least ask. And use a condom anyway.

Syphilis: Considered one of the oldest sexually transmitted diseases, Syphilis has been around for thousands of years. This disease can and still does kill many people because it often goes undetected. It is caused by a spiral-shaped bacterium. It is most often spread by sexual intercourse but can also be spread through transfusions if the blood is not tested properly. It goes through three stages, the last one being the most dangerous. Fortunately, syphilis is curable and treatable, especially in its first two stages.

1st Stage (Primary): At this stage, the disease causes a painless sore or sores on or in the genitals and mouth. This can be on the vagina or penis, anus, tongue or a woman's cervix and sometimes on a man's scrotum. The sore is highly infectious but will disappear within a few weeks. This does not mean the person is okay. The syphilis will stay in the blood.

2nd Stage (Secondary): Between one and two months later, the disease will cause a rash, swollen glands, hair loss and a number of other minor health problems. If untreated, these symptoms will also disappear in a few weeks. However, the person still has the disease and needs treatment.

3rd Stage (Latent Syphilis): The person still does not know he or she has Syphilis and seems normal, but the disease is still at work. In its last stage, syphilis can cause damage to the heart and other organs, the bones, eyes and ears. It can also cause paralysis, insanity and death. This can take years or even decades to occur, but the damage to the body is irreversible. Therefore, if you are sexually active, it is important to note any changes in your body and get them checked out as soon as possible. If you think you have syphilis, the time to get rid of it is now. Syphilis can also make you more susceptible to contracting other STD's, including AIDS.

Chlamydia and Gonorrhea: Different diseases but with similar symptoms, Chlamydia and Gonorrhea often go hand in hand. Fortunately, they are both curable and treatable. Gonorrhea is the oldest known sexually transmitted disease and Chlamydia is currently the most common. Symptoms: Yellowish vaginal discharge, stomach pain and pain when urinating, vaginal bleeding and fever.

Chlamydia: Caused by a bacteria, it can cause sterility in a man if he goes untreated. It causes Pelvic Inflammatory Disease in women (PID). Pregnant women run the risk of spontaneous abortions and stillbirths. Symptoms usually show within two weeks of infection if there are symptoms at all. One of the biggest health issues with Chlamydia is that many people, men and women show no symptoms at all. It is treated with special antibiotics. The only way to prevent Chlamydia is by using a condom.   ·

Gonorrhea: Also caused by a bacteria, it is most often detected by an infected man because his symptoms are usually the most noticeable. He will have a burning feeling during urination and a pus-like discharge from his penis. Symptoms will usually appear within 3-10 days. Many women have no symptoms at all. If left untreated, it can cause PID in women, blood poisoning, arthritis and other problems. Latex condoms can be effective protection against Gonorrhea.

Pubic lice and Scabbies (Skin infestations): Highly contagious and annoying, these two STD's are the result of pests

called arthropods. Many people are familiar with them.
Lice: Also called "Crabs", they are caused by a parasite. They cling to hair anywhere on the body and love the pubic area. It is fairly easy to detect lice because the normal human eye can see them. The female parasite lays eggs which hatch in about a week and remain near the base of the hair strand. Condoms do not prevent lice. The only way to get rid of lice is by using special shampoos containing ragweed or certain prescriptions. They live on blood and cause a great deal of itching. Lice are not life threatening, but should be dealt with immediately.

Scabies: Too small to see with the naked eye, these tiny bugs burrow under the skin and can make like miserable. Scabies is not as contagious as lice. It usually takes several encounters with someone that's infected to get them. Scabies can appear anywhere on the body and often show up in geograpghic areas where there is poverty and poor hygiene. Condoms offer no protection against scabies. They can live on furniture, clothing and bed sheets. They can also cause an allergic rash. They are treated by special creams applied to the affected areas. If you have scabies and are treated, you should also wash all of your clothes and linen in hot water and dry them. This will kill any scabies that may remain to give you problems in the future.

Vaginal (Yeast) infections and Trichomoniasis: Are conditions you can live with, but they can cause serious problems after a period of time if they're not treated. Vaginal infections, usually called yeast infections, are caused by an overgrowth of microorganisms in the vagina. These microorganisms can be bacterial or fungal. Both can cause considerable discomfort.

Symptoms include vaginal itching, thick, cheesy discharge or yellow, sour to fishy smelling discharge, abdominal pain and pain during sex. Poor diet, stress, a weakened immune system and other diseases in your body can all trigger vaginal infections. If you have sex with a man who's been with another woman that had a vaginal infection, you can get that vaginal infection. Yeast infections are usually easy to treat with creams or suppositories. Medication can be taken for either one, three or seven days, depending on the brand you choose.

If you've had a vaginal infection before and suspect you have one again, you can buy prescription strength, over-the-counter remedies that work very well. If you are noticing an unusual smell or discharge coming from your vagina and you don't know what's causing it, you should see a doctor. If you keep getting the same vaginal infection over and over again, you may need to get medicine for your man. Sometimes, the menstrual cycle is the cause. Or, you may have a weakened immune system as a result of an ailment. One symptom of HIV and Diabetes is repeated vaginal infections.

Trichomoniasis, called "Trich", is more serious than a vaginal infection and commonly spread through sex. If untreated, it can cause Pelvic Inflammatory Disease (known as "PID") which can interfere with your ability to have children. Symptoms include a yellow to greenish, very foul smelling discharge and pain or discomfort during sex.

Trichomoniasis is usually treated with oral medication (Metronidazole). Because of negative side-effects associated with metronidazole, it is supposedly better to take it in one large dose. If you have Trich, ask your doctor for the one dose treatment instead of a prescription lasting several days.

TO SUM IT UP:

Because the risk of disease is so great in this day and age, the only way to give yourself peace of mind is to take the proper steps to protect yourself and your partner. Use a condom! You can also follow the guidelines listed below.

IF A MAN'S PENIS HAS A FUNNY ODOR, DO NOT TOUCH IT! GRAB YOUR PANTIES AND SPLIT!

A funny odor can be your first sign that something is wrong with him. A funny odor is an odor that is sour, unclean, like old urine or similar to penicillin. If the odor is sour, he may be carrying the bacteria or fungus for a vaginal infection (Monilia, Gardenerella, Chlamydia, Trichomoniasis). If a man has sex with a woman who has a vaginal infection, he can pass the infection onto you. If the odor coming from his penis is unclean or like old urine, he may have poor washing habits. A man with poor washing habits carries a lot of germs. If the odor is similar to penicillin, he may be taking antibiotics for something you wouldn't want to catch.

A man should have a pleasant, musky scent, especially between his legs. While each man smells differently, none should smell bad. Your man should smell clean If the man you are about to have sex with doesn't smell clean, tell him to forget it and get out of there. Don't be embarrassed to change your mind. It's your right. In fact, it is your responsibility!

If a man you are seeing is known to be with other women, either leave him alone or use extra-thick condoms and a spermicidal cream or jelly that has nonoxynol 9.

Protect yourself! No man's sex is worth dying for and no man is worth the risk, especially if he doesn't have the sense to keep his dick in his pants. Be smart.

If a man refuses to use a condom with you, he's refusing to use one with everybody else. Stay away from him!!!

Any man who refuses to use a condom these days is not only irresponsible, he's downright crazy! Why would you want to sleep with someone like that? If you're a woman who has trouble saying "no" after things are already in motion, don't begin until you both agree you will be using a latex condom.

Purchase several different kinds of latex condoms and have them ready and available every time you plan to have sex!

This way, your man has a choice. Choosing the right condom can be fun. As you learned in the chapter on Penistry, each man's penis is unique. Experiment with different brands, sizes, styles and colors of condoms to find the most comfortable. If no condom is the only way he wants to go, he should be having sex with his own hand and nobody else.

Last but not least, be safe and **Hang Tight!**

Defecting to The White Side:

How could you and why should you?

We begin with a comparison and contrast based on a group session and written survey of ten African-American women.

BLACK MAN vs WHITE MAN

Black man = Prowess	White man = Powerless
Black man = All night	White man = All hype
Black man = Horny	White man = Corny
Black man = Salami	White man = Weiner
Black man = Silky	White man = Milky
Black man = Mandingo	White man = The Beatles/Ringo
Black man = Screaming	White man = Squirming
Black man = Satisfaction	White man = I want my money back.

Any questions?

Interracial Situations: Do they work?

Situation #1: "Mitchell." His mother was Scandinavian and his father was from Senegal. As a child, Mitchell had problems adjusting in school because he never really felt accepted. He had blonde hair, blue eyes and white skin, but the blonde hair was thick and coarse and his features were undeniably African. He was also very tall and muscular. Like that Michael Jackson song, Mitchell didn't know whether he was Black or White. He was both and he was neither. Militant and angry, Mitchell spewed hatred of White people, carried Black-Power paraphernalia and was generally an unpleasant person to be around. Although he normally wore his kinky blonde hair in an Afro and sported a nappy beard, when convenient, Mitchell would shave his beard, cut his hair very low and attempt to blend in with the Caucasians at his college. Sometimes it worked and sometimes it didn't. When it didn't work, Mitchell was very upset and confused.

During the interview with one of our researchers, he said that he sometimes resented his parents for marrying each other and having mixed children in a society where distinct racial lines do not blend. He said he identified more with being Black, but found he was often chastised by Black people for looking the way he did. He felt he could never be one with "his people."

Situation #2: "Sam." Sam, a White man, was adopted by a Black family when he was six years old. His natural mother, a close friend of the woman who adopted him, asked the Black family to accept him as a member before she died of cancer. Sam grew up on collard greens and chitterlings, could do "The Butterfly" better than most Jamaicans and spent his adolescent years dating Black girls. Handsome and pleasant, he had no difficulty attracting women. But, his attempts to date White women were disastrous. He always forgot to tell them about his "family." When Sam brought the unsuspecting women home to meet his uncle Marshall, an ex-football player with a busted leg who owned a bar in Harlem, they freaked out and refused to see him again. Sam found himself continually disgusted. He ultimately married an Hispanic woman. **Situation #3: "Tommy" and "Benita".** In love and determined to make it work, Tommy is white and Benita is black. They met at a company where both of them are working and knew instantly they wanted to be together. Tommy's family is Protestant and Benita's brothers are members of The Nation of Islam. Use your imagination on this one.

While some interracial marriages do work out, others are plagued with problems. Whether those problems are worth it depends entirely upon the people in the situation. If you are considering hooking up with a White man, also consider:

- You will be stared at in the street, depending on where you go.

- You will constantly have to deal with racism.

- Your children may have trouble adjusting.

- Your family may dislike and/or disown you.

- You may lose touch with your Blackness.

- You may never have another orgasm.

True dat, or not true dat?

On the other hand, many Sisters contend...

WHITE MEN HAVE MORE MONEY

DINEROS.
PESOS.
BANK NOTES.
POUNDS.
LE DOLLAR.

YOU NAME IT. THE WHITE MAN'S GOT IT.

They say White men can't jump, but who cares? Dollar Bill is all that. Let's face it, it's the truth! In this age of Capitalism, some Sisters feel it's better to shoot for the moolah!

So, now it is time for you to decide. Whatever you choose, considering what a lot of these Black men are doing, we think it's all good. Go for yours, Girl! Get that wampum!

And what about you? What do you think? Do you want to know how the average Black woman feels? We may have found out. We conducted an open forum with Sisters of various ages and backgrounds. What they had to say may be shocking. Maybe you'll be able to relate. Get ready for their complete candidness. We asked them: what's really up with that White/Black thang?

SOME INDIVIDUAL PERSPECTIVES

The Black women we surveyed in the group session offered these interesting perspectives:

View #1
"A man is a man no matter what color he is and besides, you can't see his color in the dark."

"Yea, but you can smell him." View #2

View #3
"White men are good at oral sex, making up with their mouths what they lack with their dicks."

"White men are really stiff, but not necessarily in the right places." View #4

View #5
"Black men fuck you. White men make love to you."

"It's an individual thing. It all depends on what you like." View #6

View #7
"If you limit yourself to just one type of man, you'll be just that. Limited."

"They say ignorance is bliss. I've never known a White man that turns me on, so I'm perfectly happy with the Brothers. It doesn't matter what anybody says." View #8

"A decent White man can be rather pleasant to have around." View #9

View #10
"I like their stringy hair."

View #11
"The White men I've dated treated me really nicely and with a lot of respect. The Black men were exciting, but there was always some problem."

"Everybody's got problems." View #12

"I think I'd prefer a Japanese man." View #13

View #14
"I don't want to be brutalized, I want to be caressed. I want to be treated like a delicate flower and I want a man to worship my body. If any man, Black or White can do that for me, I'm satisfied. The rest doesn't matter."

View #15
"White men don't have slamming power, but they can stroke pretty well if they have a sizable dick."

View #16
"I've yet to meet a White man with a really sizable dick."

"The good thing is, they (White men) don't keep you on your back too long." View #17

View #18
"They can be very thoughtful, sending you flowers and calling you often."

"They like to send you roses because they don't know where the "bud" is. The only "bud" they know is; "This Bud's for you." View #19

"Seeing that white body against your black one is kind of interesting, but after that, there's nothing else." View #20

"They look too raw." View #21

"But, I hear they're not as cheap." View #22

"I don't see what difference color makes, as long as you have someone who cares about you." View #23

"No matter how much a White man cares for you, he'll never be able to relate to what being Black is all about. How can he? How can a White man possibly understand you as a Black woman?" View #24

View #25
"Good Black men are hard to come by. Any of the single women in this group should know that. And what about all these Black guys going out with White girls? That makes the situation even worse. Don't get me wrong, I love Black men more that anything. But, things are getting crucial. I don't necessarily want to, but at this point, I'm willing to date just about anybody."

"No matter how bad it gets, I'm not going the other way. I would never disrespect my Black brothers and my race like that." View #26

View #27
"I don't care what nobody says. Black men are the ones that got it goin' on."

"I can't really speak on White men because I've never really gone there. They just don't turn me on." View #28

View #29
"White men get can get loose with a few beers in 'em."

"Do you think they fuck the way they dance? Lord knows they've got rhythm problems. Do you think they can get their swerve on, you know, like a Brother? I'm actually curious."
View #30

And yet another view:

"The more White women that date Black men, the more we'll have angry White men with money who'll be available. Granted, the Black men have bigger dicks and can fuck better. But, can that pay the rent or buy you a new fur coat? Let those White women have those broke-ass niggers. Give me the man with the loot!"

Draw your own conclusions.

ONLY JOKING

Question: What's the easiest way to get a man to exercise his
        stomach?

Answer: Put the T.V. remote between his toes.

How To Turn On Any Man: 7 Easy Steps!

7 easy steps to: Getting the man you want, keeping him and driving him crazy.

Getting the man you want is easy, once you've learned how. Throughout history, women have manipulated men in order to get what they wanted and they did it with little effort. Take Helen of Troy, for example. Legend has it that The Trojan War was fought because two powerful men wanted her. One kidnapped her, the other built a large wooden horse and staged an elaborate rescue plan to get her back. You can believe Helen knew what she was doing. If there is a man you want, you have the power to get him, provided he is not already in love. If he is already in love, you may have to choose another victim. Or, wait until the man you really want becomes single.

In this chapter, seven steps are described that, in combination, give you heavy artillery in the war to win your man's heart. Make no mistake about it. You have to be ready for mortal combat. Getting a man you want to fall in love with you, especially a stubborn man, is war. Some men guard their hearts like Fort Knox, keeping it shut tight with a huge, impenetrable door. Amazingly, all it takes is one little key to open the door. That key is the *7 EASY STEPS!*

Before you begin, ask yourself why you want to get this particular man. Is it because he's "The one"? Or, is it because he's a challenge, you can't believe he doesn't want you or you've got to get him to prove to yourself you've got skillz?

If it's the last case, be very careful. Black men do not like women who toy with their feelings. Some Black men kill women who do that. We want you to live.

If however, you sincerely care for the man and want him for yourself, then read on. After finishing this chapter, you'll be in a much better position to get him.

STEP 1: Seduce.

There are many ways to seduce a man. Some work better than others. All can work depending on how they're done. No two women can seduce a man in exactly the same way.

Although men think they're the ones to make the first move, it is usually the woman who does. By giving a man a certain look, a little smile and doing certain gestures, a woman lets him know that he can approach her. She has already begun to seduce him without having spoken a word!

There is a saying; "Men want what they *see* and women want what they *hear.*" This explains why men are always looking at other women. To grab his interest, you will have to attract him physically. This does not mean you should dress up like a hooker to get his attention, it *does* mean you should stock up on an arsenal of clothes that will make his eyes widen and his pulse speed up ten paces. Men are almost always motivated by sex. Consider the booming "Tits and Ass" industry. If you'll notice, there are topless clubs everywhere. Some men spend several nights a week in these places, squandering money, looking at professional T&A. No matter how much they deny it, their primary interest is in pussy. Get with the program. Decorate the pussy and make it enticing.

Understanding Seduction

To fully understand seduction, let us draw upon the experiences of our female ancestors and apply what has been effective from time beginning. Let's examine Cleopatra VII.

Cleopatra VII, Queen of Egypt: Not considered classically beautiful, but stunning by any standards, Cleopatra VII was a Black woman to be admired. She was seventeen when she came into power, spoke several languages and knew how to subdue a man. Any man. Her methods were simple but effective. She maximized her feminine power.

How did she do this?

The technique she used was to enhance every good feature she had while downplaying her weak points. For example, she had prominent eyes and full lips. She used black kohl around the eyes and accented her mouth using henna lip dye. In her hair, she wore beautiful jewels. She pampered her body and kept it beautifully scented. Her skin was silky and glossy. Any man coming near her was soon intoxicated.

Whenever she met a new man, Cleopatra made herself appear radiant. Her entrance was always elaborate. She wore sheer, revealing gowns, posed seductively and gave the target her most arresting stare. She was impossible to resist.

When making love, she used exotic herbs and remedies to intensify the sexual experience. Sometimes she would apply mint oil to the man's penis and then slip him inside of her. The coolness of the mint combined with the heat of her body were exquisite for both of them. She knew how to keep a man hard all night. She capitalized on the typical male weakness.

What about you?

Assess your best qualities and go to work on those. Do you have great legs? Show them. Are your breasts juicy? Wear something tight or low cut to display them. Do you have the mad round bootie? What better way to let a man know that than to wear a good pair of jeans? What about your face? What's the best part or parts? Do you have attractive hair?

The make-up you wear doesn't have to be heavy, just applied right. If you have nice lips, outline them and wear the best shades of lipstick for your skin tone. Don't wear anything too loud. In *Delilah Power,* available exclusively through Swing Street, enhancing make-up techniques for the African-American woman are fully explored.

Keep perfume soft and not too heavy. Perfume should be intimate. He should smell you when you get close. He shouldn't smell you from a block away.

Always make an entrance! Whenever you see that man, make certain to enter his space like a beauty pageant queen. Let your presence fill the room and surround him. Smile at him coyly and don't give him too much attention. Men get turned on when you show interest, but somehow ignore them. Make it challenging. Show confidence. Make him come to you.

STEP 2: Observe.

Find out his likes and dislikes. What kind of person is he? Is he outgoing, or is he the quiet type?

If he's outgoing you should focus on making him feel special. Outgoing people are very individualist and need reassurance they're not getting lost in the crowd. The more unique you make him feel, the more he'll think you recognize his individuality. This will warm him up faster than anything.

Say; "You're so different from anybody I've ever met." When he asks why, say; "Because you see things in a unique way. You just do things differently." He'll probably nod and be silent. But, rest assured. He's taking it all in and he loves it.

On the flipside, if he's the quiet type, you should spend your energy trying to relate to his way of thinking. The more connected he feels to you, the more he will grow to like you. If, for example, he has a particular philosophy about life and he expresses it to you, you should tell him you understand it, or better yet, you feel the same way. You don't have to lie or compromise your principles to do this, you're just letting him know you can relate to his views.

Say things like; "Wow. I can't believe I've finally found someone who sees it that way, too." Or, "You know, I've always thought the same thing?" He'll melt like margarine.

Is he very athletic? If so, learn more about the sports he likes and use them for conversation. You can also ask him to be your personal trainer or regularly ask his advice on diet and nutrition. This will cause him to spend considerable time with you, thus giving him ample time to get to know you. He'll also feel needed. Men want to be needed.

The idea is to become involved in whatever is important to him. When he sees your genuine interest in his life, he will be flattered. Most men can't resist flattery. If he's like most men, he'll be unable to deny the urge he feels to be around you. This technique works exceptionally well with "The robot."

STEP 3: Accommodate.

Here, you have to figure out what kind of woman he normally likes and accommodate his tastes as much as possible. If he likes the intellectual type, try to be a little more serious. If he likes to party, focus on having fun. You should not try to become someone else. Not only is it impossible, it's damaging to your self-esteem. Think more in terms of getting into new things, things he's into that you might like. If at any time, you don't feel comfortable with what you're doing, or with him, he may not be the right man for you. Find another that's better!

STEP 4: Admire.

Make him feel worthy. A man who knows he is admired is a man ready to fall in love. One of the main reasons men say they fool around is because the new woman admires them in ways their wives or girlfriends no longer do. If the man you're after knows you think the world of him, he'll be blinded by his own ego. At that point, all you have to do is lead him by the nose. Most Black men think they've got more going on than they actually do. Whether it's their sexual ability, their looks or their intelligence, they believe they're "all that." Spend some quality time and energy playing up to that belief and you'll have him eating out of your hand in no time. Guaranteed!

STEP 5: Sex.

Black men are blinded by some good pussy, especially Black men that are robots. Give him something to keep him awake nights. We will use Marilyn Monroe as an example. She was sexy, naughty and innocent at the same time. She knew how to manipulate a man. You can, too. There's a saying; "Sex is an act of nature, but it makes a man a fool. It takes away his money and wears out his tool." A sexually satisfied Black man is a happy Black man. For sexual techniques, see the chapter: *Sex with the Black man* or the book, *Delilah Power.*

STEP 6: Understand.

In the beginning: Recognize and accept the fact that men are different from us. At times, that difference will be very exciting. At other times, especially when you've gone further into the relationship, it will be unbearable. Men have different needs and different expectations. Some simple ways to keep the peace:
• Never comment on his driving.

• Don't nag him.

• Give him space, especially when he seems to be withdrawn. Personal space is healthy for a man.

• Don't get overly upset when he looks at other women. A Black man's hormones are always on auto pilot. Sometimes, he's not even concentrating on what he's seeing. To him, it's all T&A. Nothing personal.

• Laugh at his jokes. Even the corniest men like to

believe their jokes are funny. Laughter is a turn on!

• Listen to all of the stories he tells about himself. Even the incredibly boring ones. A man's favorite topic of conversation is *himself*. If you can give your guy an interested stare and make him believe you find his life intriguing, he'll be very grateful. Black men are programmed to think they own the show. Allowing them to believe they do, stimulates their circuitry.

If, on the other hand, you've already gotten the man and have been with him for a while...

So, he was like Michael Jordan in the beginning but now, he's something different. He's something you can't stand at times, something you wish you could change. You found out the hard way your man is a robot (see: The Black male machine). Chances are you're just tired of him and need a break. If you find your patience is low and you just don't have the energy to deal with him, you should probably give yourself some space. No man is perfect and they'll all get on your nerves at one time or another. Sometimes, he doesn't realize just how irritating he is to you. In fact, he thinks he's quite charming. Unbelievable, huh? It's the truth. If you keep that in mind, you may be able to refrain from lighting his ass up.

STEP 7: Maintain.
Give him a steady flow of love juice to keep his engine running. Unfortunately, after a woman gets the man she wants, she often feels she no longer has to work in order to keep him. Wrong. Men need constant stimulation, like babies. If you leave a man unattended for too long, he'll begin to cry and whine and beg for a nipple. Any nipple. At this point, the man will suck on the first nipple that comes his way.

Keep the relationship in prime shape by tuning it up every once in a while. Go romantic places. Wear sexy clothes whenever you can. Give him a back rub when he's tired. Serve him his favorite foods. Give him a big hug. Look happy to see him when he comes home. Tell him you love him. Most of all, accept him as he is and appreciate he's a unique individual.

Now for a review:
SEDUCE!
Seduce him from the beginning. Make him notice you.

OBSERVE!
Observe him closely. Make him think you belong together.

ACCOMMODATE!
Accommodate him as best as you can. Sweeten him up.

ADMIRE!
Admire him. Let him know how wonderful he is.

SEX!
Sex him like no other woman has done before.

UNDERSTAND!
Understand he is only human. Make allowances.

MAINTAIN!
Maintain your course of action. Don't give up.

Note: In order to keep your man, you must periodically go through the **7 EASY STEPS,** especially steps 1,4,5 and 6. Never let him forget why he chose you in the first place! ❄

Health and Beauty Tips for The Natural Sister

Women of color are naturally beautiful. But, we need to take care of ourselves in order to preserve that beauty. A little touch of cosmetics can help, yet is not always necessary. In this chapter we will give you some basic tips to enhance what you already have. Naturally.

Taking care of the Body

As a rule, the more natural, the better. Luckily, as a Black woman you don't need a great deal of assistance in order to look your best. Natural products are less likely to irritate your skin, have undesirable side effects or cause Cancer. However, if you are a woman with very sensitive skin or known allergies to food, you should use caution before trying any new product on your body. As always, you should check with your doctor.

Hair: You should clip your ends every six to eight weeks. Some women are afraid to cut their hair, but not clipping the ends can actually *prevent* it from growing. The ends are the oldest part of the hair and are often split and coarse. Each time you comb your hair, those ragged ends can get caught in the comb and cause the rest of it to break.

There are many natural conditioners for the hair, some of which can be found in your refrigerator. If you do not like to use a lot of chemicals on your body, these options are ideal for you. The health-holistic approach to beauty is great!

Mayonnaise: Smells funny while on the hair, but makes hair very glossy. Will wash out thoroughly. Put the contents of an entire jar on the head, wear a foil cap for 20 minutes and wash out. Follow with a cream rinse, if desired.

Sour Cream and Avocado: Blended together until smooth in a food processor or blender, these two increase the health of the hair tenfold. Use with a foil cap and/or a hair dryer on low for 10-20 minutes. Wash out and style.

*You can also rinse you hair with beer. (Don't laugh, Egyptian women did this for thousands of years. It's actually a wonderful rinse.)

Henna: Is a good product for conditioning, but has some drawbacks. It is really good only if your hair is natural. Meaning, unprocessed. Henna does not wash out, but wears away gradually. If you attempt to apply a relaxer or chemical coloring while the henna is coating the hair, you may have some problems. The henna can alter the effects of whatever chemicals you're using.

Braiding: Contrary to what many women believe, braiding the hair tightly does not make it grow faster. In fact, when the hair is constantly braided too tightly, the hair follicles in the scalp become damaged. After a while, you can become bald at the hairline or in patches and that baldness will not go away. If you suffer from bald patches resulting from too much braiding, see a dermatologist. You could also try a product which contains the ingredient Minoxodil. Products such as these can be purchased over the counter, but have shown some long-term side effects. It's wise to check with your doctor first.

If you like to keep your hair braided, it is better to have the braids done more loosely to save the hair and protect the scalp and delicate follicles. You will have to get it done more often, but it will be worth it.

If your hair is relaxed, keep scalp and ends moisturized with a good hair cream. You can minimize breakage by using satin pillowcases. As you sleep, you will toss and turn. With satin pillowcases, your hair will slide across the pillow and not break. Or, you can wear a satin scarf to bed.

The Skin: Lotions containing cocoa butter work well with Black skin. Coconut oil is also good. Plain old petroleum jelly is great for the feet. Baby oil is good for softening cuticles. **For softer feet:** This is best done just before going to bed. Immediately after showering, apply petroleum jelly, cocoa butter, or heavy lotion to the feet, rubbing it thoroughly into the skin. Make sure to massage whatever you're using into the toenail cuticles as well. Put on socks and sleep with them on. Your feet will look and feel great in the morning. **For softer body skin:** Did you know that all lotions and moisturizers are made primarily out of water? Here's a little trick to make your skin extra soft. Do not dry your body thoroughly after washing. Apply whatever lotion you use to damp skin. The lotion seals in the water, making your skin even moister. You'll be able to feel the difference once your body finally dries.

Fresh coconut oil in a jar is cheap at the supermarket and does wonders for your skin. The drawback is you must keep it refrigerated and use it quickly. It is also unsuitable for the summer because it will draw flies and mosquitoes. Mineral oil or baby oil are good choices. They can be applied alone or mixed into your favorite lotions to enhance them.

In Ancient Egypt, Black women bathed in sour milk because it made them look younger. Scientists today are just figuring out how that was possible. As you get older, new skin doesn't grow as fast as before. That's why the skin on the face and body begins to wrinkle and look dry. Alpha-Hydroxy Acids, which occur naturally in several foods (including sour milk, certain citrus fruits and sugar cane), encourage the skin to replenish itself at a faster rate. Black women knew thousands of years ago what "advanced" science is just discovering.

Because it's probably not sensible for you to try and bathe in sour milk, if you can find an affordable lotion containing Alpha-Hydroxy Acid, use it. Even more ideal, buy a stick of pure cocoa butter, melt it and mix it in with the lotion you bought. The results you achieve will be amazing. **The forgotten area:** The neck. If you do not take care of your neck skin, it will look aged. Keep it moisturized. When moisturizing the neck, as well as the face, always stroke upward with the fingertips. This lifts the skin and keeps it more elastic. **For smoother facial skin:** Do not use soap. Use a natural oatmeal bar or fresh oatmeal mixed with water in a bowl. It's messy, but it's worth it. Rub the oatmeal gently against the skin. The oatmeal naturally sloughs off dead skin, allowing new skin underneath to come through. Also, use a moisturizer that is not too greasy, preferably one containing Alpha-Hydroxy Acid.

Deep cleanse the face with natural green clay powder. Mix about two tablespoons clay powder with water or Witch Hazel, apply to face and let dry. Wash off and apply your regular moisturizer. You can also bathe in clay water to cleanse skin.

Natural aloe vera gel applied to the face helps heal blemishes and eliminate scars. Buy it in a jar from the health food store and keep it refrigerated after opening.

Never dig nails into facial skin when squeezing pimples. Use a tissue, if possible. Not only do nails cause scars, touching a pimple with your bare hand can cause you to get more pimples because the pus can be spread to other areas of the face. Avoid squeezing oil from the nose and chin. After a period of time, the pores can become enlarged and you will have craters in your face. After squeezing pimples, use a good astringent such as Witch Hazel to close pores or splash cold water on the face. Avoid rubbing alcohol. It's too harsh for facial skin.

If you suffer from acne, Tea Tree oil can become your best friend. The results you achieve are really amazing. Available at any health food store, it is applied twice a day after cleansing the face. If you have dry areas, try pure Jojoba oil. It's light, non-greasy and relieves irritation.

The nails: When nails become brittle, they break. Keep the cuticles moisturized by rubbing lotion or mineral oil deep into the skin every day and keep nails painted 90% of the time. You should allow your nails to breathe periodically by removing all polish and leaving them that way for several hours. Also rub lotion directly into the nail. File chipped nails in one direction only. Do not saw. Use a nail buffer to smooth edges.

With regards to using make-up: There are many ways to save money and still look beautiful!

What the cosmetic manufacturers don't want you to know...

Cornstarch powder you buy from the supermarket is an excellent base for eye pencils and blush. Use a small amount, rub it into the skin thoroughly and watch how long your make-up stays fresh. It also absorbs the oil from your skin and is non irritating. A box that will last you two years will cost you less than a dollar.

Baby oil is an excellent make-up remover. And it doesn't burn. It will take off waterproof as well as regular make-up. Apply liberally to the eyes and skin, see how easily the make-up comes off. Use pure cotton balls, not tissue or toilet paper to wipe the make-up away. Wash face afterwards. Baby oil also acts as a moisturizer. A large bottle of the generic brand costs less than two dollars and can last you longer than five jars of a brand name make-up remover.

Getting in shape for Sex

Whether you are having sex frequently, occasionally or not at all, your body could probably use some tuning up. Because specific muscles come into play during lovemaking, it's a good idea to exercise certain areas of the body on a regular basis (outside of bed). The more you tighten up those areas, the better you'll be *in* bed.

In this section, we will reveal a series of special exercises which, when practiced regularly will turn you into a sex goddess! Satisfaction for you and your man are assured!

No kidding! Your man will literally lose his mind! These exercises are easy, fun and give you the results you want quickly. They only take a few minutes a day.

Not feeling sexy right now? Don't worry. You hereby have our unconditional assurance that you *will* begin to feel sexy, provided you follow the instructions herein. Get ready...

You are about to go where no Black woman has gone before... to a dimension where your man can't resist you and finds himself ready and eager to please... where you achieve the ultimate pleasure and have no difficulty reaching your greatest orgasms.

You have just entered *THE SEXY ZONE!*

Before we can proceed, you must enter into a contract with yourself to follow the instructions you are about to receive. Please print and then sign your name on the lines below.

I, _____ (Print name), hereby agree to pass completely through *The Sexy Zone*. I promise to follow all instructions coming up in this chapter and devote a portion of my spare time to becoming the woman I know I can be.

X_____   _____
      (Signed)   (Date)

Congratulations! You have just committed yourself to working on becoming a more sensuous, vibrant and sexy woman! We know you can do it and we expect you to keep your promise!

If you follow our sexual regimen, you will see a dramatic change in your body. Sex will feel better and you will want to do it more often. Your man will wonder what's gotten into you and be ready to get into you, too. We have categorized the exercises you will be practicing under three basic goals:

Goal #1: Increase your flexibility. The more limber and flexible you are, the more sexual positions you'll be able to do. You'll be a tigress in bed. Do you want your man to roar?

Goal #2: Increase your stamina and power. The stronger you are, the longer you can last. And so will he.

Goal #3: Strengthen and tighten the vaginal wall. Learn to use your little cat in ways that will drive him crazy. Need we say more?

Sounds good, doesn't it? Now that you know what to expect, take a deep breath and read on...

GETTING READY

When in The Sexy Zone, wear something comfortable such as sweat pants, a tee shirt, spandex, or very loose fitting jeans. Try not to do the exercises from our Sexy Shape-up program on a full stomach. A great time to work out is in the morning, before you've had your shower.

Put some sexy music on. Maybe some Sade, Luther or R. Kelly. Get yourself into the mood. You've got to *think* sexy. Find an open space somewhere in the middle of the floor and make sure there are no no obstacles in your way. Stand firmly, feet spaced apart. Take ten deep, slow breaths to increase the flow of oxygen to your muscles and relax them. Raise your arms slowly and lower them ten times. Breathe. Now...

Goal #1: Flexibility.

Stand upright with your feet comfortably spaced apart. Let your arms hang at your sides and roll your head around slowly. Keep shoulders still. Do this four times. Reverse direction.

Now, roll your shoulders up and around to the back four times. Make big circles. Do this slowly. Reverse direction.

Drop your chin to your breastbone. Hold 10 seconds.

Swing your arms back and forth eight times and then twist your upper body from side to side. Try not to move your feet. Do this several times and then shake your legs out to loosen them. Now, you're ready for action.

Fig. 1.1: Here, you stretch out your calves while finding good position of the back. Keep the body as far over the front leg as possible yet keep the chest lifted. Try to feel a stretch in the thighs.

Now, straighten the back leg and press the heel to the floor. Breathe deeply, stay for 3 seconds then bend the back leg again as in figure 1.1. Do this 10 times and then change legs. (Fig. 1.2)

In Fig. 1.3 at left, the hips are raised as high as possible from the floor.
Push pelvis up to the ceiling in a smooth and rolling motion. When you achieve maximun height, hold for 5 seconds and then bring body slowly back to floor. Keep 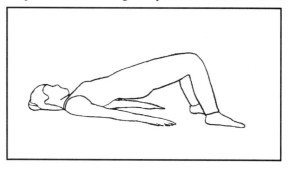 knees bent. Maintain steady breathing. You should feel buttocks and abdomen clenching. Do not strain the neck. Repeat pelvis push 10 times.

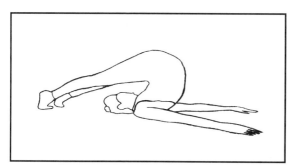 Fig. 1.4: If you can achieve this exact position, do so for 10 seconds. If you cannot, lie on your back and hug your knees tightly to your chest for a few seconds and then release them. Now, stretch your legs up to the ceiling, knees as straight as possible. Arms down, palms on floor. Hold 10 seconds.

Fig. 1.5: Keeping one leg straight and as close to the floor as possible, breathe deeply and pull the other bended leg into the chest, knee up and in. Hold 5 seconds. Switch to other leg. Do 8 times each leg, making sure to shake legs out.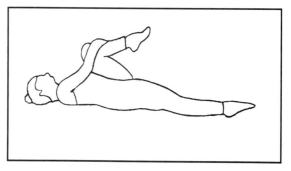

Goal #2: More Power!

The following exercises will strengthen the thighs, work the hips and stretch the back. Combined with a sensible diet, they do wonders for the sex life. Streamline it! Go for yours!

Using an ordinary broom...

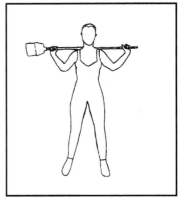

Fig. 2.1: Stand with feet spaced apart (a little more than your hip's width), and place broomstick over your shoulders. Keep both legs straight. Grab stick in two comfortable places and twist body from side to side, keeping hips as still as possible. Your body should remain vertical. This exercise loosens the waist, works the back and hips. Breathe normally as you work out. Each twist counts as "one." Do this fifty times. If you cannot do fifty, do as many as possible. Increase daily.

After you have done this, you will work on stretching the back and thighs. You need a strong back and powerful thighs when your man is banging you out doggie style, especially if he likes to do it standing up. Keeping legs straight, bend over to a flat back and twist body from side to side. Slowly touch the end of the broomstick near your left hand to your right foot and vise versa. Do this twenty times. Increase by five each day until you can do fifty. After that, continue with fifty.

Fig. 2..2: Squat. This exercise is a thigh buster. Once you master this, you will be invincible when you sit on your man and ride him. Go down slowly, head up and counting to five until you are as low as you can go. Come up quickly. Repeat. Begin by doing this twenty times a day and increase by five every other day until you can do fifty. You will be amazed in no time. Continue with fifty.

Goal #3: Tighten up!

Learn to use your female sex in ways that will drive your man crazy! Rule #1: The more you can control your female organ, the more you'll be able to control your man.

Here are the exercises that will give you the control you need.

Working the Vaginal wall

While sitting or lying down, do the following:

a) Concentrate on the vaginal area and tighten it as you would when stopping the flow of urine. Hold it tight and count to 10. Release. Do this 10 times.

b) Next, tighten the vagina while sucking in the abdomen. Hold for ten seconds and release. Do this 10 times.

c) Bear down through your stomach and vagina as if you are having a bowel movement. Focus on contracting the abdomen at the same time. Hold 3 seconds. Repeat 10 times.

Do the entire sequence everyday, twice a day.

Another terrific way to tighten things up is to increase abdominal strength by doing sit-ups and leg lifts. If you're like most women, you probably hate doing stomach exercises. So, forget about those unless you really want to do them. We'll show you a technique that's fast, easy and will make your grip as tight as a fist. Once you've got your man in a solid grip, you can hold onto him for as long as you want!

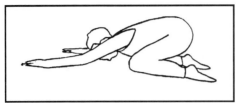

Fig. 3.1: This stretch re-
leases the back, the thighs
and hips. Relax in this
position for about 60
seconds.

Rise onto all fours (Fig. 3.2).
Pulling the stomach in, arch your
back up like a cat. Keep head down.
Do this slowly and breathe. Hold
for a few seconds.

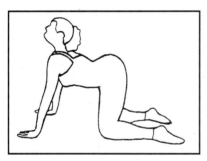

Now release. Reverse the arch so
that head is up, spine is swayed.
Press shoulders down away from
ears. Alternate and repeat both
arches 10 times. (Fig. 3.3)

Fig. 3.4 (next page): We call this position *The Tribal Pump,* because you
assume a position often held by primitive tribes in other countries. This
position will make you unstoppable. Once you have achieved the position,
try bouncing up and down 25 times. Make the bounces small. If you can do
more than is suggested, by all means. The more the better. When you have
mastered The Tribal Pump, try doing it while having sex with your man.
Watch what happens to him.

   Caution: If you find that you are getting tired while exercising, be sure to
give your body a rest. Remember, Rome wasn't built in a day. It takes a

while to become a sex goddess. Do as much as you can everyday and even-

tually you will be able to do more and more. Most importantly, don't let your man know what you're up to until you are completely equipped and ready to rock his world with your new technique! Let's hope he can handle it! ❖

For those who want to work the tummy:

Hold this position for 10 seconds. Relax and repeat 16 times. If you want, you can continue with a regular sit-up set (Fig. 3.5 at right).

For the very daring...

Once mastered, the three exercises

below and at left can dramatically increase the potential of your body while having sex. Only attempt them after you have fully warmed up and completed all other exercises in The Sexy Shape-Up Program.

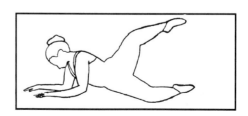

Open and close 24 times, each side.

Diet and Nutrition

The following recommendations are suggestions only and are not to be confused with or considered as strict guidelines for nutrition. Before undergoing any drastic changes in your diet, you should consult your doctor.

Good foods vs Bad foods

Contrary to what the diet books tell you, it is okay to eat the things you like, as long as you don't eat too many of them. And you don't have to exercise everyday to have a healthy body. But, you do need to exercise sometimes. If you just can't make it to the gym on a regular basis, try walking up the stairs to your apartment once a day and walking to any location that is less than ten blocks (or a half-mile) away.

Water in the diet can go a long way. It flushes out impurities, clears up your skin, makes your eyes brighter and keeps you healthier. If you can't live without soda, it's not a sin. Try substituting water for soda at least one meal a day. It can make a real difference.

Foods to cut down on: Tea and coffee with caffeine, butter, whole milk, fried foods and fast foods. Roasted nuts are a diet killer! Cake and ice cream are okay if you only have a reasonable amount. If you're one of those Sisters that can go through a pint of ice cream or a whole 9" cake in one night, it's time to go through sugar detox. Buy the tiny cup of ice cream and one of those tiny cakes for $.79 instead.

Foods to increase: Fruits and vegetables, lean meats (chicken and fish) and home cooked foods without a lot of butter or grease. Go light on gravy and avoid chicken skin. Bananas are good for the diet because they're filling, loaded with vitamins and cheap.

Use non-stick cooking sprays whenever you can. Cut down your sugar and salt intake. You don't have to go cold turkey, just try to avoid adding salt to your meals once they're prepared and don't add sugar to corn or sweet potatoes when cooking. Eliminate those unnecessary calories!

Note: If you are on an exercise regimen, trying to firm up, you must reduce your fat intake. Fat in the diet converts to fat on the body as well as cholesterol in the blood. As a woman, you naturally have more body fat than does a man. Cut the fat and watch those muscles firm up fast. Try eating lower fat cheeses, spreads and sweets. Also use lowfat mayonnaise.

CONCLUSION: You are a Queen!

Assuming your rightful position as Queen.

YOU ARE A QUEEN! Before you read any further, repeat these words aloud. **"I AM A QUEEN!"**

And you are! Despite slavery and the injustices of this country, we retain the lineage of magnificent kings and queens and are destined to do great things. Although some of you may not realize it, you have the power to do whatever you want with your lives and become just about anything. Why is it, then, that so many Black Women end up feeling worthless? In this final chapter, we shall discuss the reasons behind the feelings of helplessness some Black women have and give you solid methods for improving your self esteem.

HISTORY REPEATS ITSELF

As a slave, a Black woman was violated by her White masters, stripped of her dignity and told that she was ugly. She was denied feminine comforts and was forced to do grueling work for long hours. Her beautiful body, beat down by years of abuse, would deteriorate until she was only a shell of what she once was. Still, the Black woman remained proud, keeping her family together and constantly struggling against the odds.

Today, Black women are still told in subtle ways that their natural beauty is not good enough. The black woman is told she must conform to a European standard of beauty in order to be acceptable. Longer, straighter hair and tons of make-up are what she needs to get a man. Although more and more Black models appear on the runways, the women chosen to represent the Black race are often not true examples of the diverse beauty we possess. So, what is a Black woman to do? Fortunately, there are sisters out there who, proud of their natural beauty, choose to grow locks, install braids and keep their bodies free of too many cosmetics. In Ancient Egypt, Black women did enhance their looks with natural products such as Henna, Kohl and scented oil. Even if you are a Sister who relaxes the hair, we give you props. Chemical relaxers can make hair care a lot easier when you're on the go. Still, as a Black woman, be aware that it is very easy to fall into the trap of trying to look like the White women on television. Not only is it impossible, it says a lot about your self image. Enhancing your self esteem is what we are going to address in this chapter. It's time to work on you!

YOU ARE BEAUTIFUL!

There is a saying; "Believing is half of being." What this means is, if you believe in something, you're already half way there! If you don't feel attractive, you will not be. If you believe you are beautiful, men will buzz around you like flies. How many of you have seen a woman whose face wasn't that pretty, but who always seemed to have the attention of men, fine men, men with money? Have you ever stood there in awe, unable to figure it out? We surveyed a number of men and arrived at the following conclusions:

Many men recognize inner beauty and are attracted to women with high self esteem, regardless of how they may physically look. When a woman is in high spirits, she glows. When she loves herself, she shines. This glow and shine is felt by any normal man and will cause him to respond accordingly.

A woman that feels good about life and herself will attract men because they want to feel the way she feels. They feel good in her presence. She brings out the best in them. **Women who take care in their appearances are very attractive to men, regardless of their actual physical features.** What does this mean for you? It means you have the power to be as attractive as you wish. All it takes is a little belief in yourself. The first step is cleanliness. Clean hair, fresh breath and teeth and clean clothes are all attractive to a man. Skin that is soft (use lotion everyday) is also pleasing. Manicured nails are a plus although many men like the natural look. Try to find a hairstyle that is flattering on you and keep it neat. Use make-up that calls out to a man and doesn't shout at him. **Men love women that smile.** Remember that song; "I love your smile?" The fact is, everyone likes to be around pleasant people, especially men. When a woman smiles, her face is inviting. Men love invitations. Most Black men can't resist them. If you want to attract a Brother, hit him with your most seductive smile. Even if he's unavailable, watch how he reacts to that smile. He can't help himself. The best part about a smile is, you don't have to go to a beautician to get one. They're absolutely free and you have enough of them to last your entire lifetime! Why not spread them around?

So, now what?

There's a way to feel better about yourself! Begin by acknowledging that life isn't perfect and things may not always go the way you want them to. Just because you've had a bad day doesn't mean the world is against you or you're less of a person. And if you're in a bad mood, don't feel guilty about it. Everyone is entitled to a bad day and to make mistakes. What's important is that you continue working for the things you want and try to stay optimistic. You'll find there's a reason why things don't work out sometimes. It's usually because something better is on the horizon!

Start with you! Forget about all your problems for the moment and put together a list of all the things you have to be thankful for. Do you have someplace to live? If you do, you're lucky. Even if it's not a fancy place, it's better than nowhere to live at all. It's no fun being homeless. Put that high on your list of things to be thankful for. Do you have people around you that love you? Do you manage to eat every day? In a world where people are literally starving to death, being able to eat is something any person should be thankful for. Are you relatively healthy? Are you completely sane and intelligent? If you are reading and understanding this book, you must be. These are all things you can be thankful for.

> The longer your list gets, the more you will realize that your situation is not so bad after all. Once this happens, you will feel much better about your life. Try it. It works!

Make a list of your qualities. Forget your faults.
Everyone has good points. Everyone. Make a list of yours, from the fact that you can be a thoughtful listener to that you're a good cook. What's your talent or talents? Everyone has at least one. Some people never discover theirs. If you don't know what your talents are, think of the everyday things you're good at and list those. Being nice is in itself, a talent!

Stop comparing yourself to others! If everybody in the world was the same, it would be a pretty boring place, wouldn't it? Accept and acknowledge you are a unique person with your own set of experiences. Who cares what the other people are doing? It's up to you to make the most out of your life. No one else is responsible.

Make a list of all the things you've done, have always wanted to do and how many of them were

accomplished. Big or small, everything you do is worth something. Have you raised your own children or someone else's? Did you graduate from high school or complete a career training course? What about college? Have you remained true to your religion? These are all things to be proud of. Do you work, keep a clean house, or help out an elderly lady in your building? What about the things you do for your church? Are you kind to stray animals? Even the smallest act of kindness is worth putting on your list.

Begin by learning to hold your head up high, even when you don't feel like it. Look at your posture in the mirror. Are your shoulders hunched, your chin held low? Try to consciously stand straighter whenever you remember. A straight spine lifts up the body and makes it look much more appealing. It doesn't matter whether you're thin or heavy, short or tall. When you stand up straight, your body looks better. After a while, you'll even feel better.

Start taking care of your body! When you take care of your body, your body will take care of you. If there are some things you know you should be doing for better health, what are you waiting for? Old habits die hard, but you can overcome them if you take that first step. Sometimes the best things are the ones you really have to work for. What better way to get revenge on that man that dissed you than by showing up one day looking your best? He needs to know what he's missing. Having trouble getting started? Most people procrastinate. Don't be too hard on yourself if you tend to do it sometimes. But, don't keep making excuses either. You've got a lot of inner strength. Use it. And see if you can get one of your friends to join you in your quest for a healthier body. It's fun and you can keep up with each other's progress. If you know it's time to start exercising... *JUST DO IT!!!*

When you begin to take care of yourself, you begin

to feel better about yourself! You are the only thing you have in this world until you die. Your body is all yours and you can do whatever you want with it. If you take care of it, it will take care of you. *You're* in control. Remember that.

Start getting rid of the things that are unhealthy for you. Whether it's a man, a job or a habit, start working on getting rid of anything you feel isn't good for you.

Sometimes it's more difficult to get rid of things we don't even want. This is because we're often afraid we won't find anything better. We will, if we give it a chance. If you're unhappy with your job, start looking, asking around and keeping your eyes open. If you hear of something that seems good for you, check it out. Even if you don't get it, the fact that you're looking will make your present job easier to deal with. You know in your heart you're leaving soon, after all, you *are* looking, so that bitch you have for a boss is less of a headache. Also, she's probably got her own problems.

What about your man? Is he dogging you out again? Start collecting phone numbers from the interested men you meet. If you feel like calling them, call them. You're not breaking the law. It's just nice to hear some new nonsense for a change. Note: Don't leave those numbers around the house or anywhere your man can find them. That's asking for trouble. Even if you love your man, knowing another man wants you is sometimes enough to help you deal. After all, you could be with someone else if you wanted to. The numbers you've collected prove it. It's smart to keep your options open.

Learn how to say No! One of the most difficult things for a Black woman to learn is how to say no. By nature, a Black woman is considerate and accommodating. She cares about people and wants them to be happy. She also hates conflict and will try to avoid it if possible. She will help someone else pursue happiness at the expense of her own. She is very sensitive and has a conscience. This is her nature.

The only way to learn to say no is by practice. You don't owe anyone an explanation for exercising your right to say no. When you explain yourself, especially to a Black man, you give him undue power over you. And you seem weak. You're not weak. You're a strong Black woman, right?

If a man asks you for something and you don't want to deal with it, simply tell him "no" in a nice way. If he's a robot and used to getting his way or hearing explanations, he'll likely push the issue. Ask him in a non-confrontational tone to respect your feelings and accept you cannot help him at that particular time. He may get angry, but his anger will pass and in the end he will respect you. Despite himself, he will become more obedient. Eventually, he will be reprogrammed.

Start doing more of the things you like to do. It's time to start investing more time and money in *you.* If you re-budget your money, you'll find you have a little more to spend on things you'll like a lot better. It's easier than you think.

Begin by taking a good look at your budget. For one week, keep an accurate record of all the money you spend. You'll probably find you're spending a surprising amount on things you don't even need. Some of you will find you actually throw money away. Next, decide which things are absolute priority and which things can be replaced by something else.

Choose something reasonable that you've always wanted to do. We stress the word "reasonable." If you're currently earning minimum wage, you shouldn't be thinking about Yacht racing or any other expensive hobby. Maybe you've always wanted to join a gym or learn how to paint. What about Karate? Or poetry? There are a lot of places that offer all sorts of classes free or practically free.

Broke? Why not volunteer? Helping others is uplifting to the spirit. Get involved in a fund raiser for your favorite charity or participate in a walk, marathon or event to raise money to fight a disease. Meet people, feel wonderful and get in shape!

At the end of this chapter is a listing of institutions which offer free and affordable courses in a variety of areas. Many of them will send you a free catalog if you call them.

If you can't think of anything you'd like to do right now, take that money you've budgeted and get a new haircut or a new set of clothes. Or buy yourself a good book (such as this one!), a new CD or get a make-over. Whatever you do, use that money for *yourself*. You'll look good and feel good.

Start making time for yourself. Time is one of the things you'll have to *take* for yourself! No one else will give it to you! When you have a job and/or children to deal with and/or a man, finding time for yourself can be a difficult thing. Have you ever felt people sometimes have no consideration for your feelings when you're tired and need a break? That's because people generally don't consider the value of your time. They love you, but they want what they want and they want it *now*. That's why it's up to you to make them respect that special time you've set aside for yourself. Even if it's only 30 minutes a day, make a decision to give yourself that block of time and don't answer the phone, don't answer anybody's questions and definitely don't let anybody bother you. There are very few things that can't wait 30 minutes.

Even if you do nothing for that 30 minutes, you'll feel great knowing you decided to take care of yourself for a change. You'll be in better spirits.

The more time and energy you invest into yourself, the better you'll feel about yourself!

Taking care of yourself is beneficial to all aspects of your life and other people. You'll be happier in your relationships, have more patience for your children, you'll interact more with others and be more content overall. Now that you know what it's going to take to be a better you, why not start today? You have the rest of your life to become the kind of woman you know that you should be! Let's get busy! ✪

GREAT IDEAS FOR GREAT EXPERIENCES

The New York City Department of Parks and Recreation has programs operating at centers in every boro. For only $25.00 a year, you can join their centers and use their gyms, pools, weight-lifting equipment and take classes such as Karate, Aerobics, and Dance. The centers have state-of the-art equipment and clean locker rooms. You can't find a better deal in the city. You'll also see fine brothers playing basketball and lifting weights.

> The New York City Department of Parks and Recreation
> 16 West 61st Street
> New York, NY 10023   (212) 408-0100

The New School offers a range of courses at very affordable prices (some only a few dollars). They have just about every class you can think of from Boxing to Pottery. Definitely worth checking out. For more information:

> The New School
> 66 West 12th Street
> New York, NY 10011   (212) 229-5600

The Learning Annex is a center that has some interesting things to offer. The classes are inexpensive and fun. There may be a small registration fee.

> The Learning Annex
> 116 East 85th Street
> New York, NY 10028   (212) 570-6500

The Museum of Natural History: Pay what you want to get into the museum building. They offer free classes year round as well as free performances in dance, music and drama from all over the world. Put your name on their mailing list and they will send you schedules.

> The American Museum of Natural History
> Central Park West at 79th Street
> New York, NY 10024   (212) 769-5315

New York Open Center gives free open house sessions that include lectures, demonstrations and refreshments. Seriously into developing your mind and body? Check it out. It's an interesting place for the adventurous.

The New York Open Center
83 Spring Street
New York, NY 10012 (212) 219-2527

The **Learning Alliance** has workshops, festivals, language classes, literary readings with well-known authors and more. You pay a sliding scale fee.

Learning Alliance
324 Lafayette Street, 7th floor
New York, NY 10012-2726 (212) 226-7171

Rising Spirits Healing and Learning Center, Inc. is a not-for-profit organization which focuses on growth and mental healing. Psychotherapy and support to families, particularly women and their children.

Rising Spirits
540 West 55th Street
New York, NY 10019 (212) 399-1873

The Central Park Conservancy: Located at The Arsenal, in Central Park. Environmental and visitors programs. Free weekend family workshops, exhibits and the like. A great way to spend quality time with the kids. Call:
The Charles A. Dana Discovery Center at (212) 860-1370
Belvedere Castle: (212) 772-0210
The Dairy: (212) 794-6564

The Job Corps is an employment training program for people aged 16-24. Vocational programs, basic education and social skills development.
Job Corps
17 Battery Place, 20th Floor
New York, NY 10004 (212) 363-1336 or (800) 733-5627

* If you live in another city or state, contact your local Parks Department, Museums and Cultural Affairs offices for information on free or inexpensive programs. Other good sources of information are your local newspapers and supermarket bulletin boards.

Minding your own Business:
Do you want to be The Boss?

Many Black women dream of having their own businesses but don't know how to begin. Starting a business is not as complicated as you might think. It *does* involve a tremendous amount of leg work. Owning and operating a small business requires dedication, determination and perseverance. Most small businesses fail within the first two years due to improper planning. If you have ideas for a business and wish to explore them, it would be wise to solicit help from a professional before you go into debt or invest a lot of money. At the end of this section, you'll find a listing of organizations which can help you gather most or all of the information you'll need. Some of them are dedicated to helping minorities. If you take time to research, you will find a number of resources.

The first thing you should do in your quest to become self-employed is decide what type of business you want to start and investigate the field. Ask yourself: Is there a good market for the product I want to sell, or service I wish to provide? Where will my business be located? How much money will I be able to invest initially? How much money can I afford to lose? Starting a business means risking money and possibly going into debt. Think it through carefully. Many African-American women are establishing their businesses at home, a perfectly legal and cost-effective way to get started. There are tax ramifications however and you will probably need the services of a good accountant at tax time.

The procedure for starting a business is generally this: you first establish the legal structure of your business by obtaining a business license or certificate. This is done through the County Clerk's office and costs about a hundred dollars. Call or stop by for the exact price and more information. There are three basic types of businesses: a "Sole Proprietorship", a "Partnership", or, a "Corporation". Each has advantages and disadvantages for the small business owner.

Sole Proprietorship: You own the business and keep all profits, but you are vulnerable to lawsuits and the loss of your personal assets. You make the full investment, assume responsibility for all debts and are fully at risk. This type of business is usually less costly to start and maintain than a corporation. You can even begin the business at home and expand to an office as your success grows. If you are just starting out or have limited money to invest, a sole proprietorship may be the logical choice. Your tax liability is lower and you preserve your control over the venture. You can also tailor the business to suit your specific needs and work at your own speed.

Partnership: You enter into business with a partner. This is a very risky option. Business partnerships are known to destroy friendships. While a business partner supposedly shares the investment and takes equal financial risk, he or she can ruin you and the business by embezzling money and failing to live up to his or her responsibilities and commitment. You are legally bound to consult your partner on all business matters. If you decide to forge ahead with a business partnership, draw up a clear, written agreement outlining your responsibilities and commitment to one another. Legally, a business partnership is as contractual as a marriage. The only way to rid yourself of a partnership is to completely dissolve the business. Afterwards, you are free to count your losses and start over.

Corporation: In simple terms, you structure the business so that your personal assets are protected. In effect, you shield yourself legally by becoming an *employee* of the business you establish. You make money by paying yourself a salary for work you do and you collect your portion of the profits. Ownership of the corporation is based upon the number of "shares" or percentage of the corporation that you and other people (if there are any), own. In this case, you can take on a partner with less personal risk. The corporation is supposedly run by a board of directors and the profits are distributed between the people (called shareholders) who own the shares.

However, an individual can legally own a corporation, be the entire board and sole shareholder. People sue the corporation, but not you. If the business goes into bankruptcy, your personal assets and credit rating are safe. Running a corporation is expensive however, and subjects you to a double tax situation in certain instances. You generally need a lawyer's help to become incorporated. Oftentimes, it is not cost-effective for the new business owner to structure her business in this way. Still, if you begin your venture as a sole proprietorship, you should eventually consider changing to a corporation as your business expands and legal issues become more complicated.

Following is some general information to assist you. Keep in mind the less money you have, the more leg work you'll have to do in order to establish yourself and your business. It won't happen overnight and you will find the voyage rough at times. Try to pace yourself and don't hesitate to ask friends and family for advice and support.

Write a business plan. The first thing you should do is write out a basic and informal business plan. A business plan will arrange your thoughts and provide a preliminary blueprint of your entire business. Eventually, it will become your means of obtaining financing and credit from lending institutions. There are specific ways to construct a business plan, but you can worry about that later. For now, you just need to organize your ideas. One approach would be to categorize your concepts and concerns. Use several sheets of paper. On one page, you can list the details about the business as you imagine them (the name, desired location, types of clients you intend to serve, known competition, etc.). On another, you could jot down the supplies and materials you'll need to get started. One page could be used to assess your finances (how much money you currently have, your debts, what resources are available to you, money could you borrow) and still another page could be used to outline a simple marketing strategy (how, where and when you will advertise, your budget, etc.), and so on. With a plan such as this, you will be better equipped. The Small Business Administration has a free publication which can help you write the business plan. See the end of this section for more info.

Attend courses, seminars, lectures and conferences. Many organizations give free or inexpensive courses in business, accounting, etc. Whatever you pay is tax deductible. Call the organizations in the listing on page 148.

Join trade organizations. Trade organizations keep you abreast of what's happening in your field, offer support and referrals. Trade publications, also good sources of information, can be purchsed at most magazine counters and book stores.

Confer with other business owners. If there is an establishment in your area that is similar to the one you want to start, visit the owner one day and request an interview. Most people are proud to talk about their accomplishments. You can also use that time to gather information on organizations, contacts, manufacturers, etc. All it will cost you is time.

Following is a checklist of items you will probably need for your business venture. All items are fully tax deductible as business expenses. Retain receipts for everything and keep a log of purchases and expenditures.

Business Essentials

A computer. This may be the best thing to invest in first. Your computer will become your personal secretary, banker and accountant. You will use it to track sales, inventory, clients, as well as access The Internet. It is an invaluable tool for the small business owner. Get the best computer you can possibly afford. Don't buy in haste and make sure you're not paying for features you don't need. There are a number of magazines which rate computer equipment. Ask someone who knows about computers to help you make your choice. With wise spending, your cost can be a thousand dollars plus and the purchase will be tax deductible.

A Postal Box. For roughly fifty dollars a year, you can use a postal box as your mailing address until you procure an office space. In order to use a P.O. box for business, you must present your business license to the Postmaster. Because people are skeptical of businesses with P.O. boxes, list your address this way: use the Post Office building address and put the # sign in front of your box number. For example: Get on Top Press, 226 West 33rd Street, #540. You will still receive your mail and your address appears to be an office.

A fax machine and/or fax modem. Using a fax machine or modem is a convenient, professional and inexpensive way to conduct business. A fax machine can cost under three hundred dollars and a modem can be much less. A modem is necessary for downloading files from The Internet.

A business bank account. A business bank account will legitimize your business, help you build credit and allow you to keep your personal banking and finances separate. The service charges for the account will start at about twenty dollars a month. Shop around for the bank with the best rates. In general, the large commercial banks are more expensive.

Business cards, stationary and flyers. You may be able to create these yourself, using your computer. Print shops charge fifty dollars and above for several hundred, professional looking business cards. Don't bother with machine-generated business cards that cost five dollars. They look cheap.

Business-related software. Consider purchasing a few word processing, accounting and legal software programs to assist you in the operation of your business. Software packages can cost under a hundred dollars apiece and should be sufficient for your needs. Some may come installed with your computer.

A 24-hour electronic voice mail service. Or, if you can afford it, a live answering service. Prices can run as low as fifteen dollars a month for electronic voice mail and forty dollars for live service. Do not use a pager number as your business number. It makes your business appear shady.

A second phone line. If you plan to conduct business at home, an additional phone line will be useful when accessing The Internet. Your personal phone will remain free. A second phone line in a home-based business is fully tax deductible. **An E-Mail address and/or Web site.** Almost every business has an E-Mail address and/or Web site. Web sites can be expensive, but E-Mail addresses are relatively cheap. If possible, have your business cards printed with your E-Mail address. Comparison shop for Internet servers and pick a provider which offers high speed access to The Net at no extra charge.

Feel ready to take the plunge? Contact the organizations listed below and get a copy of your local Business to Business Directory. Read up! Also check out the book, *Delilah Power.*

The Small Business Administration (SBA): (212) 264-4354. Free advice and publications. Ask for a start-up kit.

SCORE (Service Corps of Retired Executives): (212) 264-4507. Free counseling on a walk-in basis.

UBAC (Urban Business Assistance Corporation): (212) 995-4404. Low-cost consulting and business courses.

The Minority Enterprise Development Program: (212) 264-4322. Information on resources and various funding for small, minority businesses.

The Division of Small Business: (518) 473-0499. NYC Regional Office: (212) 803-2319. Info, workshops, etc. Call for an information packet.

New York Magic: (212) 696-2442. Services the small business. Free business counseling, help securing financing and more.

Small Business Development Center: (212) 346-1899. Based at Pace University. Services, information and resources for small businesses. Technical Assistance.

Interracial Council for Business: (212) 779-4364. Additional resources for the minority business owner.

Finding Mr. Right:
Overall Comments on Test Questions

Question 1: You should never tell a man you just met where you live, *especially* if you live alone. If he asks, give him a vague address: tell him the general area. If he persists, tell him you don't make it a habit to tell strange men where you live.

Question 2: The best way to meet a man is through someone else you know or a work, school, etc. It is easier to compile verifiable information on him. Also, in the event your new friend ever does something crazy, other people know who he is and what he looks like.

Question 3: You should not invite a man you recently met into your home, *especially* if you live alone. It is not a good practice. Did you know that roughly 80% of all rape cases are date rapes? The victim usually knows and mistakenly trusts the rapist. Go out on dates to public places and let people you know see the two of you together and let them meet him.

Question 4: A lot of men lie about themselves. Check out as much of the info he gives you as possible. When he takes out his wallet to pay for something, casually ask him to see his driver's license picture. One of the women we interviewed dated a man whose name was different from what he told her. He turned out to be a convicted child molester.

Question 5: If a man calls you a lot, it only means he likes you. It doesn't mean he can be trusted.

Question 6: You should always know as much of a man's sexual history as possible. Remember, when you sleep with a man, you're sleeping with everyone he's ever had sex with. And condoms are no guarantee against certain diseases.

Question 7: The only time you may be able to tell a man has a disease is if he has full-blown AIDS, genital warts or active Herpes. Otherwise, he may look perfectly healthy.

Question 8: A man will usually show signs he is lying. The information you received in the chapter on finding Mr. Right should help you recognize those signs. If you still need more assistance, purchase the book, *Delilah Power.* If you're not certain of his intentions, keep your distance.

Question 9: Mysterious men are intriguing, but only to a degree. Forget James Bond, he's only good in the movies. You need to *know* where your man has been and what he's in the habit of doing. It's only wise.

Question 10: There are a number of men out there who can make you happy. Just keep your expectations realistic.

Question 11: Honesty is definitely the best policy.

Question 12: A bad seed usually has a funky odor. If you sharpen your senses, you will be able to sniff out a bad seed in a minute. Bad seeds cover their intentions with a crocodile grin, but they always give themselves away. Reread the chapter on Finding Mr. Right and the chapter: The Sucker Syndrome.

Personal Test Results
(Based on pages 41-43)

50-60 Points: You are a woman with a lot of common sense and use caution when considering a new man. You know what qualities to look for and do not make hasty or rash decisions. You've had your share of ups and downs, but you learn from your mistakes and probably have fulfilling experiences with men. You go, Girl!

40-50 Points: Although you have good common sense, you may tend to ignore your instincts. You need to check that. You sometimes take calculated risks. When meeting someone new, look more closely for the warning signs. In terms of your relationships with men, you have a decent chance of getting involved in a good one. You're not often taken advantage of.

30-40 Points: You're an intelligent woman, but you take dangerous risks with men sometimes. You probably find yourself in situations you have trouble getting out of. You rely too much on luck. Remember, luck always runs out. If you want to remain in good health, you should consider changing your approach to relationships and even make some lifestyle changes. If you can, approach your mother for advice when you are unsure of someone. Although mothers don't always tell you what you want to hear, the advice they give is usually sound. Who do you think cares for you more: the person who gave birth to you, or a man who could have everything to gain by deceiving you? Give it some serious thought.

20-30 Points: You seem to have little idea of what's really going on in the world today. If this is true, you need to start facing reality before it's too late. It will probably take a bad experience for you to open your eyes. Hopefully, that experience will not be life or health threatening. Although you seem to have a fairly good head on your shoulders, you often forget to use it. Why not take a good look at your behavior and make a change today? We hope you do it before it's too late!

0-20 Points: Do you enjoy living dangerously? You appear to be wrapped up in some fantasy world and will find yourself in deep trouble one day, if you haven't already. It is only a matter of time. Your score indicates you have no sensible thoughts of the future. You also neglect to consider the consequences of your actions. You should pay closer attention to stories that are being reported daily in newspapers and on television about women who become victims. If you enjoy playing Russian Roulette with men, that's your prerogative. Your expectations are unrealistic and you probably don't even realize the danger you tend to put yourself in. Forget about finding "Mr. Right." You should not be a relationship, you should probably be therapy. Have a long talk with your mother or get in touch with a close female who's an older woman. Show them this test and your results. They'll school you.

If you are in need of therapy... There are a number of organizations that can help you. Check with the Mental Health clinic of any city hospital, ask your medical doctor for a referral to a therapist or you can call your local information number and ask for the listing of a mental health hotline.

ONLY JOKING

Question: Why is psychoanalysis a lot quicker for a man
than a woman?

Answer: When it's time to go back to his childhood, he's
already there.

Some food for "Thought."

Little Ricky was sitting in Math class when his teacher called upon him to answer a question.

"Little Ricky," she began, "Imagine there are four birds sitting on a fence. If you shot one of them, how many would be left?"

Little Ricky thought about it for a moment and then he answered; "None. The noise from the gun would make the rest of the birds fly away."

The teacher smiled. "Actually, the answer is three," she said, But, I like how you're thinking."

After class, Little Ricky approached the teacher. "I have a question for you," he said, "There are three women in an ice cream parlor. One woman is licking her cone, one is biting her cone and the other is sucking her cone. Which one is married?"

The teacher chewed her lip nervously for a moment and then she finally replied; "I guess the one who's sucking her cone."

"Wrong," Little Ricky replied, "It's the one wearing the wedding ring. But, I like how you're thinking."

❋   ❋   ❋

Is your mind on the money?

Solve this riddle and see just how well you know your "Mean Green". If you had to make sixty-three dollars in change ($63.00), using six bills and no singles, how would you do it? You can use any combination of bill denominations, but no singles. The answer is on the back of this page.

(1) Fifty-dollar bill, (1) five-dollar bill and (4) two-dollar bills = $63.00

This and That!

Odds and ends for your use.

Look 'em Up!

Need to find that deadbeat dad? That lost love? Those relatives or friends you lost contact with and miss so much? Finding someone can be a lot easier than you would expect.

If the person you are looking for lives within the same city as yourself, you may be able to locate him or her by going to City Hall. First, jot down as much as you can remember about the person and then go to work. Do you know the person's date of birth? Social security number? Last known address? Check the hall of records and the county courthouse. All of the data retained in these offices is public information.

Here are other ways of finding someone who is deliberately hiding from you:

The Bureau of Vital Statistics: Will disclose information on a person's birth, death, marriage, etc.

The Post Office: will supply you with the name, address and/or forwarding address of any individual box holder. Fill out some forms, pay a small fee and wait a period of time for the information you need. You have a right to information concerning a US Postal Box Holder under The Freedom of Information Act.

The Registrar of Voters: Can give you information on a person's age, address, job, etc., provided the person you seek is a registered voter.

The Census Bureau: Don't rule it out. Hey, you never know.

Credit Bureaus: Do you have an attorney working with you? What about someone with a legitimate, registered business? Why not request a credit report through that business? You can find out a great deal about someone via the credit reporting agencies. Try Experian, Equifax, Dunn and Bradstreet, etc. Your fugitive may be found before he or she even gets a fair chance to turn around.

The DMV (Department of Motor Vehicles): Can supply you with vehicle identification, driving records and ownership records.

Does the fugitive have personal or real property? Check your local tax collector. You may find records of tax payments that will reveal a person's whereabouts.

Local colleges and Universities: Contact the alumni office. They will verify a person's degree, time of attendance, etc.

Another possibility... The internet! Take advantage of the latest technology. Many government agencies now have online addresses at which you can access certain information. Call your local government offices and inquire. Another possibility are the online yellow pages and telephone directories offered by the various search engines. If you are familiar with The Web and use it regularly, tap into the search engines and see what you can find. You may be surprised.

*   *   *

Other miscellaneous stuff on The Net...

For those of you who spend time surfing The Net, we have provided some additional waters. Listed are a few websites which you may find beneficial and entertaining. Enjoy!

Business Related

www.businesscreditusa.com Can provide you with current information on millions of U.S. businesses. This could be very helpful if you are researching a company. Free credit reports on businesses and low-cost company profiles.

www.bizwomen.com A good choice for networking. Search of this site will uncover some useful information pertaining to women in business.

www.entrepreneurmag.com The website of Entrepreneur Magazine. At this site, you can design your own business cards, stationary, letterhead, etc. at reasonable cost. You can also download free business forms.

www.hispanicbusiness.com An informative website created by Hispanic Business Magazine. Contains many items of interest for Latinos in business.

www.visa.com/smallbiz This website has information on local and national business organizations to join. You can also obtain information on loans, minority business programs, etc.

www.fodreams.com The site of *Women in Business Cyberspace Field of Dreams*. Here, you can locate information on general business issues. While at the site, take a moment to check out the Bizwomen's Research Directory. Another route would be: **www.fodreams.com/home.html**

www.athenet.net Provides links to professional women's sites. You may also come across a number of tips regarding starting up, running and managing your own business.

Personal

www.bigblackbook.com   A comprehensive directory of African-American businesses nationwide. You can search by state for the particular information you need or simply browse to locate relevant items.

www.socialstep.com   A popular site for African-Americans. Many items including: Upcoming Events, Business, Travel, Social Scene, Cultural Horizons and more.

www.what2read.com   An online bookstore created just for us. At this site, you can read reviews on a number of titles, peruse stimulating articles and locate other useful information.

Get online and get in shape!

www.primusweb.com/fitnesspartner: Advice from certified trainers based on current research.

www.intelihealth.com: Johns Hopkins Health Information site. Post a question via email and an expert will reply. See the area entitled: Fitness Zone.

www.worldguide.com

Genre newsletters and magazines:

Fantasy: **www.autopan.com**

Romance: **www.dreams-unlimited.com**
            www.theromancereader.com

When You're Feeling Blue...

Once upon a time, there was a rebellious little Bluebird who refused to fly south for the winter. He hung around until late November when, the weather became so cold, he realized he had to fly south, or die. Shortly into his journey south, ice began to form on his delicate wings. He struggled to make it, but he eventually fell to earth in a barnyard, almost frozen. A cow wandered by and crapped on the little Bluebird. The Bluebird thought it was the end. But, the manure warmed him and defrosted his wings. Warm, happy and able to breathe, the little bird began to sing. Just then a large cat came by and, hearing the chirping, investigated the sounds.

The cat cleared away the manure, found the chirping bird and promptly ate him.

The moral of the story:

1. Everyone who shits on you is not necessarily your enemy.

2. Everyone who gets you out of the shit is not necessarily your friend.

3. If you're warm and happy while caught up in some shit, keep your mouth shut!

*   *   *

Mama's Got a Brand New Bag!

The Righteous Mother
presents

Sit on It!
*The Pocket Companion
to **Get on Top!***

Bold. Audacious. Electrifying!

Take Your place and Take Control!

Summer 2000

Available exclusively from Swing Street Publishing.

Staying on Top!

Some final words of encouragement.

So, now you are on top! Congratulations! You've identified your goals, mapped out a game plan and set about changing your life with fierce determination. You should be very proud of yourself!

As with anything worthwhile, you will be required to work continuously toward achieving your goals. You will be tried and tested at every step along the way. As you arrive at each new level, you will be confronted with a new obstacle. Tell yourself you can achieve, and you will. Following are some practical considerations to help you persevere.

Maintain realism.

The first thing to do is develop a realistic attitude about what you are planning to achieve. For example, expecting to change your body in a week and suddenly be in terrific shape when you've been sedentary for a long time is just not realistic. If you want a better body, you'll have to make a long-term commitment to revamping your lifestyle. You don't have to live like a monk. You *do* have to moderate your intake and increase your physical activities. Ask yourself; Where do I want to be in six months? What can I achieve week to week? How can I monitor my progress on a monthly basis?

Just as fad diets don't work in the long run, neither will putting all your hopes and energy into some quick fix to change your life. Real change takes time. Give yourself time.

Maintain positivity.
Positive energy feeds on itself. What can you do to keep the positivity flowing?

Praise yourself every chance you get.
Give yourself the praise you deserve. You will need praise in order to remain motivated. Unfortunately, you may not always receive recognition from the people who mean something to you. In fact, the people you care about may criticize you when you least want or need it. When this happens, counteract by telling yourself how proud you are of what you are doing. If you have a setback, don't chastise yourself. Instead, try to make up for the lapse and praise yourself for your efforts. You will find it easier to resume your plan and you will not falter as quickly the next time around.

How many times have you had the following experience:

You set a goal for yourself. You spend a considerable amount of time and energy pursuing that goal and you feel terrific about what you're doing. Positivity abounds. Then suddenly, you find yourself in either Scenario #1 or Scenario #2.

Scenario #1: One day, for no reason you can explain, you climb out of bed and it hits you. You think; "Wait a minute. I can't do this! It's too hard! There's no way I can manage! Forget it! I'm a failure!" Or, you think; "I really want to be positive, but not today. Today, I feel like shit."

Today quickly turns into tomorrow, tomorrow turns into next week and before you know it, you've completely gone off the track. Now, you're feeling rather depressed and disgusted with yourself. Forget positivity!

Scenario #2: Something totally out of your control prevents you from sticking to your regimen or plan. It makes you angry and anxious, but you have to fulfill your obligation to someone or something else. Duty calls. You rise to the occasion, but a part of you, the part with all the wonderful plans, resents the interference. You suddenly feel disgusted. Disgust mutates into lack of motivation. Now, you have a real excuse to flush your wonderful plan down the toilet. So, you do.

There is a price, however. You are now obligated to kick yourself emotionally. You know you shouldn't give up, but there are so many barriers. Barriers are a real pain in the butt. Who wants pain? Give up. That would be easier, wouldn't it? Why even bother? What is wrong with you?

Answer: Probably nothing.

In all likelihood, you've just had what could be referred to as a minor setback. Everyone has them. It's how you handle a setback that makes the difference between success and lack of achievement. We do not use the term "failure." You simply cannot "fail" as long as you keep trying. No matter how many times you get set back and how long it takes to recover, you will achieve some level of success at every stage of your growth. It is the effort, not the result that matters the most.

Now, let's go back to those two scenarios and explore some practical ways to deal with them.

Scenario #1: "The unexpected Blahs".
"The unexpected Blahs" can be attributed to any number of things, from changes in the weather, to a restless night, to an undetected or impending illness and/or physical condition.

Plan of Action: Hunt the source of negativity down like a bounty hunter and annihilate it.

Step 1: Check the date. The first thing you should do is check your calendar. The PMS monster could have its nasty claws locked into your sensibilities. This is not a facetious statement. Many women hurdle through a myriad of emotions just before their periods. This can have drastic impact on a diet or exercise regimen. If PMS has you by the bra straps, you can relax and blame it all on the hormones. A couple of painkillers, some warm herbal tea, 48 hours and you're in the driver's seat again. No problem. Another mood killer for mature women is menopause. Many women suffer from mood swings and hormonal imbalances during this time in their lives. If you are reaching menopausal age, discuss your concerns with your medical doctor. He or she will be able to tell you if there is medication or a procedure to help ease the transition.

Step 2: Do a self-check. Ask yourself what is going on around you in your life. Perhaps you're upset about something at the job. Maybe you have a family matter on your mind. Could a love situation be cause for concern? Oftentimes when we are stressed about daily issues, we unwittingly allow the stress to transfer itself into negative energy. This negative energy filters into the subconscious and interferes with positive thought processes. Before you know it, all those great things you were planning to do suddenly seem too difficult. Your motivation is compromised and it becomes a lot easier to throw in the towel.

What is really stopping you from moving forward? Once you have identified a potential source of interference, you can look for solutions and work to keep negativity at bay.

Step 3: Do a health-check. Outside of your general mood, are you feeling physically okay? Long bouts of the blahs could indicate a deeper level of depression, a chemical imbalance or a physical ailment. If you just can't seem to shake that negative mood, you should probably discuss what is happening with your medical doctor. You could even have an allergy to something you're not aware of. Sometimes, a simple diet change can dramatically improve your emotional state.

While there is no cure-all solution for "The unexpected Blahs", you have the power to persevere. Feel comfortable with your moods and allow yourself to feel lousy every once in a while. There's nothing wrong with you just because you happen to be in a bad mood. The sun has to go down before it can come back up. Tell yourself you will continue with your plan, despite the fact that you may have lost time or a bit of momentum. Rome wasn't built in a day. Don't let something you have control over take control of you. Don't let anyone or anything stop you from achieving your goals.

Scenario #2: Uncontrollable Circumstances.
Just when you least expect it, expect it. We are all familiar with Murphy's Law. Why do we always get set back when we were just getting so far ahead? Does anyone really know?

Life is unpredictable and unfortunately, tragic at times. There will always be trials, tests, setbacks and disappointments. No matter who you are, where you come from, your economic status or appearance, you are not exempt from the realities of life. Some of those realities can hurt profoundly, but they are what ultimately build you as a person. You will achieve strength. And wisdom. And if you can make it through those impossible times, you will emerge as a better person.

Plan of Action: Grab the bull by the horns and hang on for dear life!

Step 1: Stop being a victim. You have a real say in how your life goes. Once you realize and accept your power to make positive change, you can do almost anything. Are you helping to create your own destiny, a destiny you truly desire?

Destiny is a union of happenstance and individual intent; part chance, part your own doing. To think you have no control whatsoever over your destiny is to give in to your fears. Fear can and will cripple you. Like a debilitating disease, it will eat away your confidence and prevent you from moving forward. The only way to conquer fear is to meet it head on. The more you believe in yourself, the weaker your fears will become. As you grow in strength, you find it easier to control your fears.

Which is True?

Real courage can be defined as either: a) Having no fear, or b) Having fear, but taking action despite that fear.

The correct answer is (b). Conquer your fears and you become invincible. There is no greater feeling than knowing you have accomplished what you have set out to do. Strive to overcome the obstacles. Create your own fantastic destiny.

Step 2: Forget about trying to control everything. There are times when you will just have to relax and go with the flow. While we generally know we can't control everything, we still tend to want to control too much. There is a balance between what you can and cannot control. When you try to control too much, you upset that balance. If you use common sense and judgment, if you listen to that "Inner Voice", it will be easier for you to identify the things you can and can't control.

Now, decide that it is time to fall in love... with *yourself!*

You are the most lovable person you know. Begin to get reacquainted with the one person you'll be living with for the rest of your life. Everything about you is wonderful. Enjoy who you are and let life embrace you. If you can do that, life will present its greatest gifts to you!

INDEX

About the names behind the book...

The Righteous Mother, a native of Costa Rica and raised in the United States, has spent many years helping Black women deal with their relationships. Working first as a medium and later as a personal advisor, she has used her many years of experience, psychic skills and vast insight to help women find solutions to problems both big and small. After decades of successful readings and personal advice seminars at her home in Long Island and upon the urgings of clients and her co-author, Sister Shakeefa, she decided to write this book. She is a mother of six and grandmother of thirteen. Wanting to further explore her spirituality and ancestral heritage, The Righteous Mother returns periodically to her native homeland and conducts studies there.

Sister Shakeefa was born in the United States, but has roots in St Croix, Bermuda and The Carolinas. Intrigued by the countless stories of disgruntled Black women she heard over the years, she considered writing a book which would somehow address their issues. She began an independent research project that would evolve into the book you are reading right now. A traveler and adventurer, Sister Shakeefa developed a number of surveys which she conducted during her voyages in different countries. Convinced that Black men are the same all over, she held interviews, compiled data and incorporated her findings. She met The Righteous Mother by chance and knew it was destiny. Sister Shakeefa believes this is the book every Black woman has been waiting for. Her goal is to help the African-American woman succeed. She also intends to write a book for Black men who are seeking positive change and improvement in their lives.

Cleopatra is a graphic artist and desktop publisher living in New York. More of her work will be appearing in the future.

Swing Street Publishing
NYIM
215 West 104th Street, Cathedral #846
New York, NY 10025

SURVEY

Dear Reader:

Thank you for purchasing this book. As part of our ongoing efforts to satisfy you, we have included this brief survey. Please take a few minutes to fill it out after you've finished reading the book and return it to us. By giving us your input, you make it easier for us to provide you with the resources and information you need. Also, feel free to write to us at any time or visit our website at: www.goswingstreet.com. We'd love to hear from you! We appreciate your support and hope you've enjoyed your purchase.

Name of Book: _____

1. Did you find this book entertaining? Yes_____ Somewhat _____

No_____ No opinion _____

2. Could you relate to its contents? A lot _____ Somewhat _____

Not much _____ Not at all _____

3. Did you find this book informative? Very _____ Somewhat _____

Minimally _____ Not at all _____

4. Are you planning to take any of the book's suggestions? Yes _____

No _____ Don't know _____

5. What was your favorite chapter(s), if any? _____

_____

6. Are you currently involved with someone? Yes _____ No _____

7. Are you happy in your relationship(s)? Very _____ Usually _____

Sometimes _____   Rarely _____   Never _____

8. What would you say is the biggest problem with relationships today?

_____

_____

_____

9. In what age group are you?   18-25 _____   25-30 _____   30-40 _____

40-55 _____   55+ _____

10. Would you recommend this book to a friend?   Yes _____   No _____

Undecided _____

    Do you have any additional comments about this book? What types of information would interest you in one of our future publications? Let us know in the space below.

_____

_____

_____

_____

_____

_____

Name (Optional) _____

Address _____

_____

Delilah Power!

Tannis Blackman

* Keep reading for an exciting preview
of the book, *Delilah Power!*

Delilah Power! is for every woman in the world who is out there, searching for something. Although each woman's quest may vary, the rewards harvested by reading this book remain the same. Every woman has some degree of Delilah in her. And every woman can benefit greatly from *Delilah Power!*

Open yourself to the Sensual Pleasures of an Ancient Power.

Do you know the ancient legend of Samson and Delilah? Why was Delilah so powerful? Who is 'Delilah' in this modern day and age? Delilah is a conqueror! She conquers all because she is all woman: pure female with nothing to prove, except to herself and everything to gain. She draws her strength from within, using positive means and knowledge to attain her greatest desires. She has that thing called *Delilah Power!* You now hold the power in your hands. With this book, *Delilah Power!* is yours and all you'll ever need!

From Hair to Lair: Perfecting The Art of Seduction

From the moment you catch a man's eye, you are in a position to win his heart. A simple look, the right look, can set the stage for making him yours forever. In this chapter, you will master the art of flirtation, provocative ways to capture a male's attention and keep it. Your skills will be cultivated with lessons on irresistible body language, visual stimulation and using your voice as an incredible enticement ploy. The rules of seduction are clear. You will also become skilled in the power of illusion: fully aware of how the right cosmetics, clothes and hairstyle can evoke whatever sentiment you desire. You're a hardworking woman. Now, it's playtime! Tempt him, tease him, intrigue him, or fill him with longing. The choice and luxury are yours!

Exotica and Erotica
*When Heaven and Earth become one
and Pleasure becomes The Principle*

Just how powerful are the six senses? Read on. Did you know that certain aromas, sounds and tastes are virtually guaranteed to excite the average man? *Exotica* and *Erotica* concentrate on intensifying romantic pleasure by utilizing a variety of erotic stimuli. You will become a clever mood magician: mysterious, seductive and sexy. The male will surrender himself to you eagerly, prone and at your full command. He will crave the moment when you bring him to his peak, as only you can. When a male is at his peak of arousal, burning hot and blinded by his passion for you, he will go wherever you lead him. His stimulated senses will inspire a masterful performance and he will thrill you beyond imagination.

Here are just a few of the tools you will have in your incredibly tantalizing collection:

Sexual Love Potions.
Secret Powers of Water and The Sensual Bath.
Aroma Remedies.
The Touch Effect.
Fantasies, Foreplay and Enchantment.
Channeling Crystal Energy.
Incense, Candles and Oils.
The Sweet Flavor of Love (Food as an aphrodisiac).

Men Sex and Relationships

No matter what you say or do, men will always be men. This can be fantastic, or it can be disastrous, depending on your outlook and how you choose to handle the opposite sex. Discover:

❀ Why men really *are* easy to deal with, provided you learn to understand them.

  *Delilah Power!*

- How to have a profound, loving relationship with your man. One that lasts!

- How you can achieve the most incredible orgasms each and every time you have sex. With absolutely no faking!

- How masturbation leads to self-empowerment. And sexual fulfillment.

- Ways to explore your sexual fantasies without any inhibitions and/or shame.

- How to give and receive the most cherished expression of love!

Practica and Completion

In order to survive and thrive in the new millennium, women of color must strive to achieve inner and outer cultivation. *Practica* and *Completion* address the trials and tribulations of everyday living, as well as skills and knowledge you need to maintain health and increase prosperity. The goal is success! What can you do to promote a healthier, happier and more prosperous you? Read these dynamic, information-packed chapters:

Money Madness
Black, Proud, Aware!
Mind Over Matter
Health Wealth (safe dieting/real physical fitness)
Sexy Aging
Dealing with doctors, hospitals and HMO's.
Tips on parenting for the caring mother.

Delilah Power! contains much more information than could be contained in this short preview. From starting a business, to buying/repairing a car, to understanding your strengths as a consumer, *Delilah Power!* has it! A wealth of enlightenment awaits you in this one, amazing book! Indulge yourself!

 Thank you very much for previewing this book. To obtain your personal copy of the Delilah Power! Millennium Edition, please refer to the information below and use the order forms on the following pages. Or, log onto our website: www.goswingstreet.com to place your order online.

Delilah Power! by Tannis Blackman.
The Millennium Edition
264 Pages with illustrations.
ISBN: 0-9652540-4-6 / **$11.95**

Mama's got a Brand New Bag!

The Righteous Mother™ is back: Straight from the motherland and ready to kick ass!

First, you had to Get on Top!™

GET ON TOP!

The Righteous Mother

Now, it's time for you to...

Sit on It!™

Sit on It!™ *A Queen's Guide to Life on the Throne*
The "Mother" of all Sequels!
The new book
by Bestselling Author **The Righteous Mother**™

Now, YOU can be up there, looking down and lovin' it! This book tells how you can get ANY man to assume the position: eyes wide, mouth watering and at attention... until YOU say when! **Sit on It!**™ *A Queen's Guide to Life on the Throne* shows you how to take your rightful place and reign as you should – keeping them where they belong & loving you for it! Find out what the great queens of history knew and why the queen who'll **Sit on It**™ ALWAYS rules!

"The throne is yours for the taking...
If only you would **Sit on It!**™" – The Righteous Mother™

Get Yours! Independence Day 2002

About Swing Street

Swing Street is an African-American owned and operated company, dedicated to providing information and resources to people of color. We have many upcoming projects and would love to tell you about them!

In The Works...

Sensual Poetry!   **Fiction!**

Newsletters!

Terrific Sponsors!

Author Chat!

And more!

* Write for free samples.
Free sample offer based on availability.

**What in the world is
Sen-Suá™?
Find out soon!**

Interested in meeting us? Tell us about events in your area.
Who knows? Swing Street gets around!

Call or write us for a brochure: **1-888-GO-GIRL 1**
(1-888-464-4751)

**Swing Street Publishing, P.O. Box 846 Cathedral Station,
New York, NY 10025-0846**

Or, visit our website at: **www.goswingstreet.com**

Order Form

Call **Toll Free: 1 (888) GO-GIRL 1**. 1 (888) 464-4751. AMEX, VISA and MasterCard accepted.

Postal Orders: Swing Street Publishing, P.O. Box 846, Cathedral Station, New York 10025-0846. Tel: (212) 969-8122. Send Check or money order payable to: Swing Street. Visit our website at: www.goswingstreet.com

Please send the following books:

Cost:

_____

_____

_____

New York residents must add 8 1/4 sales tax.   **Sales Tax:**   _____
Allow 2-4 weeks delivery. Include S&H.
Shipping: $3.00 first book, $1.00 each additional.

Shipping: _____

Total: _____

Payment (circle one): Check /Money order   Major credit card

Type of credit card: _____

Name appearing on card: _____

Card number: _____

Expiration date: _____/_____

Cardholder's Signature: _____

Mailing Address: _____

_____

_____